Fulfilled!
The Art and Joy of Balanced Living

Be Fulfilled!
Jacquie Hood Martin

Jacquie Hood Martin
www.jacquiehood.com

NuVision Media, Inc.
www.nuvisionmediainc.com

Jacquie Hood Ministries
Chicago, Illinois

For more information, visit our website:
www.jacquiehood.com or www.rolandsmartin.com

Subject headings:

CHRISTIAN LIVING
INSPIRATION
SPIRITUAL RENEWAL

Cover Design: Kenon White, Chicago, IL
Cover photo: Powell Photography, Chicago, IL
Layout: Kenon White, Chicago, IL

ISBN: 978-0-97191-071-3

Advance praise for Fulfilled!

"You are a Divine Diva and one of the many who give divas a "good" name? Thank you for your encouraging words."

LaRita Shelby, Author
The Nature of a True Diva, Los Angeles, CA

"When I think about all the times I have frustrated myself, trying to make things happen because I wanted them to happen, I see now how to do things differently. We need a spiritual revival and renewing of our minds to live according to the ways of God."

O. Anderson,
NBC Affiliate, Dallas, TX

"I have often felt unworthy to do things and participate in the church and community. I now see that my experiences may well help. I am moving each day toward fulfillment in my life."

Charmaine Nash

"Only God can explain why things happen. In Fulfilled! I have discovered the importance of living each day to the fullest. And for that I am grateful."

Everett Mickelson

"I have often made mistakes as it relates to decision making. I have decided as the Law of Commitment indicates to acknowledge God before making any decisions about my life. I am going to put God first and wait on Him."

Gwen Lardy

"Thank God for you. I used to keep my feelings inside because I felt so unworthy and unappreciated. I can now voice my views and opinions without feeling self-conscious."

Deon Davis

"Thank you for doing what God has called you to do. I have been struggling with the spirit of fear, but I can now move forward in achieving my intended purpose in life. I am spiritually healthy. I am whole. I am free from mental bondage!"

Dawn Lione

Fulfilled

Contents

Appreciation and Acknowledgements

My heartfelt appreciation is given to my husband for his vision, love, prayers and support. Roland, I respect and admire you for your unwavering faith and walk with the Lord.

To mama and daddy, Harriett and Emanuel, thank you for raising me to embrace each opportunity as it presents itself. To my sisters, Jennifer and Jhoslyn, and our nephew Jeremy, I am glad we have unity. May you always weigh your options, seek the greater good in your decisions, and proceed accordingly.

To my mother and father in-law, Emelda and Reginald, Martin, Sr., thank you for teaching your son the value of priorities, because you did, our household is blessed. To the Barnes family, thank you or teaching me to never compromise my principles and to continue to keep God first. To the Hood family, thank you for loving me and accepting me unconditionally.

To my Pastor, Ralph Douglas West, Sr., of Houston's Brookhollow Baptist Church (The Church Without Walls), thanks for being my father in the ministry and sharing your wisdom and knowledge of God's word. Thank you for extending me the opportunity to serve, sharing my gifts of preaching and teaching. To The Church Without Walls family, thank you for trusting and following my lead.

To all who purchase the book, see the book or hear that I wrote a book and will say, "I know her," my sincerest thanks for your years of prayers and support; for certain the prayers of the righteous are effectual.

"Beloved, I pray that in all respects you may prosper and be in good health, just as your souls prospers" 3 John 2

Jacquie Hood Martin

Foreword

So many people are in search for answers that will lead them to their dreams. The fast-paced world that civilization has evolved into causes many to look for the answers outside of themselves.

The search for balance, peace and happiness during these turbulent times is a common struggle that is heard regularly. The answers to these life questions can be found in a daily journey whose goal is to awaken the spirit so we can see clearly. This daily discipline of seeing can help us navigate through the many day to day decisions that we have to make about our time, our relationships, and ultimately, our legacy.

Recently, I asked a young medical student why he had decided to embark on this career. He responded, "It is what makes me feel fulfilled, a oneness with the universe." The clarity of his path was a powerful reminder of the spirit within.

The weaving of stories and scripture with no nonsense, everyday suggestions, makes Fulfilled! The Art and Joy of Balanced Living a life guide that you can use whenever you need support and inspiration. I have personally found Jacquie's words and concepts to be very helpful in conversations with loved ones about trusting in the spirit, and letting go of habits that limit you.

Living a fulfilled life is about putting your faith in God into action. My daughter and I recently had a revelation during a tennis practice. It dealt with putting your faith into action.

She was not playing well. We took a water break and I asked her how she felt about her play. She said that she felt frustrated, with no motivation, and not able to relax. I asked her, "What will you do?" She said, "I am praying for God to help me, but I cannot feel my spirit right now. I just don't feel it," she said in near tears. I put my arm around her and whispered in her ear, "Sometimes you have to trust that God is always there and your job is to believe and do what you need to do. That is what faith is: believing even when you cannot feel the spirit and then acting in that belief."

It was one of those moments where the spirit was present and we felt fulfilled.

Jacquie Hood Martin is a seer who has a wonderful gift and who has devoted her spirit to inspiring and sharing with others. Fulfilled! The Art and Joy of Balanced Living is a book that touches the spirit within as a powerful practical guide that encourages, inspires and assists in our journey to living a life of spiritual fulfillment.

Let the spirit guide and bless all on the path of seeing.

Rafael Gonzalez is a nationally recognized corporate trainer and mentor trainer for UNITY Journalist of Color.

Introduction

"How come you always seem so at ease?" I am told many times a day. "Your voice and demeanor is always pleasant." I tell them that I learned through many heart-wrenching experiences and letdowns how to pace myself and enjoy the journey. There have been days when I was coming unglued at the seams, and no matter how many times, I read *"be anxious for nothing, but with prayer and petition present your request to God"* (Philippians 4:6), I would still fall prey to anxiety, stress and the anticipation of things that often times never occurred.

In *Fulfilled! The Art and Joy of Balanced Living* you will quickly discover you have to take responsibility, own and embrace all of your experiences in order to fully appreciate and comprehend how your life is and has been shaped. In this book you will find eight key principles that will help you in your quest for balance and fulfillment.

A principle and a biblical law are synonymous in practice - each requires obedience. A biblical or spiritual law is defined as God's instruction to His people on how to love Him, themselves and others. It equally shows us how to manage life. And to obey or disobey that law will have either positive or negative consequences.

Understanding the application of these keys will open your mind and renew your sense of purpose. Spiritual health is just as important as emotional, financial, social, and mental well-being. You will discover how to balance your life, while changing your outlook, as scriptural teachings are applied to day-to-day stresses and stress factors.

I will share my trials and triumphs in hopes to free you from your own anxiety. Each principle presented is birthed from my own encounters with the Almighty God.

The key is discovering how to handle stress and addictions so they do not handle you. Stress is a silent adversary, and a tool of the enemy. And, long before you recognize its presence, it has grabbed your life and taken it hostage!

As you meditate on these spiritual truths, seek to put them into practice. May you be, *Fulfilled!*

Personal Statement of Affirmation

I am a free Spirit yielded only to the will of God.

I am a woman of purpose.

I am a woman of passion and compassion.

I am not susceptible to others burdens or poor personal outlook.

I am aligning myself with positive, spiritually grounded people.

I am a child of God and with Him I am untouchable.

I am a person of peace; I bring peace to others.

I am a woman with a calm spirit; I live to please God and God alone.

I believe in my gifts and myself.

I am achieving my dreams.

Jacquie

Journaling for Personal Growth

At the end of each principle you will be given an opportunity to journal. The journal is designed to work on three critical areas of interaction we have on a day-to-day basis: your interaction with yourself, God, and others. You will discover the joy of walking closer to God, while finding harmony in your relationships.

1. List a personal quality you are learning about yourself. This may be an attribute, quality, characteristic or phrase that summarizes your feelings about a particular event that has been going on in your life.

2. List two positive words of affirmation to speak into your life. Write what you anticipate to happen in your life from these words. For example: If you say, "I am a strong person and am capable of achieving my dreams." Then you will follow this statement with an outcome you expect because you are admitting to yourself you will not allow anything to hinder your path to fulfillment. For example: "Today, I will use my mind to rise above my circumstance, rather than emotionally respond."

3. List three people you come into contact with or the names of three people who you will encourage today. Purposely seek them out in order to enrich their lives with your self-discovery.

The Law of Perception

"Delight yourself in the Lord, and he will give you the desires of your heart." Psalm 37:4

Order Matters

I live for God. If you missed it, let me repeat it. I live for God! It needs to be understood that I'm not confused about who I am and whose I am. All that I do in my life is about fulfilling the will of God for my life and glorifying Him.

It is critical to understand this because when it comes to living a balanced life, order matters. The Law of Perception means that I don't perceive God to only exist in my life when I get in trouble. My goal is to do His will and depend on Him in all that I say and do.

> *when it comes to living a balanced life, order matters*

Everything that we do has order. The seasons change from fall to winter to spring to summer. In Ecclesiastes 3, we are told that there is a *"time for everything."* Our seasons in life will change from joyous to sad to worrisome to victorious. Laws govern our daily life, and there are rules and regulations that we are to follow on the job, in society, and at home.

But the order I'm talking about isn't law and order, but the role of prioritization. A balanced life is a life of structure built on a firm foundation. Our heavenly Father is a God of order and not chaos. So if we are going to live in balance with ourselves, our God, and our world, we too must have order (12 Corinthians 14:40). What is your priority structure? Is it your faith? Family? Career?

We all have different value systems based upon how we have been raised and nurtured. Some of us were raised in homes where everything was about the work ethic and nothing came before the demands of the job. Others have lived in households where a premium was placed on leisure instead of work. In my home there is no confusion.

And what I've discovered is that our priorities often tell the story as to whether or not we live a joyful life or one mired in frustration.

As you take a hard look at your priorities, I'll let you in on my personal conversation with God:

- **Who is God?** God is the head of my life, and based on my belief system the one who created me and will guide me toward Christ-centered living, rather than self-centered living. I am able to think for myself and make decisions based on biblical teachings that give me sound instructions on how to co-exist with everyone and everything around me.

- **What is family?** Family is the unit to which we are bound and sworn to uphold and love. Through birth or adoption, the family unit provides us with human instruction, companionship, and spiritual nurturing.

- **Careers are by choice!** The sooner you accept that a career comes and goes in stages, the sooner you will be able to balance your entire life. My husband once heard a woman say, "My job is my life!" He responded by saying, "So if you get fired do you die?" We seemingly have placed career ahead of everything in this money-driven society. It is the equivalent of putting the cart before the horse. Cosmetics mogul Mary Kay Ash, who led an army of entrepreneurial women in building a billion dollar company, was fond of saying, "I'm a woman who puts God first, family second and career third. I do not believe that life can be lived in any other order." She could have easily made earning money her top priority, but Mary Kay Ash knew that placing God first would make all her dreams a reality. When we see that our self-worth is not wrapped around a job, but that a job is simply a tool to manage the expenditures associated with living, we can come to terms with the fact that the more we acquire the more we work. On the flip side, the less we want for needless things the less we have to work.

My fiancé (who is now my husband) and I discussed where we were headed in our respective paths with God and openly mapped out what it would take for us to excel in marriage and ministry. Let me repeat that: we didn't discuss our career goals and what we hoped to achieve on the job. We first put God's will for our lives on the table, instead of our will. Scripture tells us *"to choose this day who you will serve. You cannot serve two masters"* (Matthew 6:24). Once we all recognize that we must operate in God's will, we can begin the process of having a more meaningful and balanced life. We are *"to love the Lord our God with all our heart and with all our soul and with our entire mind and with all our strength"* (Mark 12:30). Every part of our being is to be engaged in serving God in an uncompromising manner. In our discussions the words "I" or "my" did not enter into the conversation. From the outset, it was all about "we," "our" and 100% "us."

Through evaluating your finances, looking at debt and acquiring only what is necessary, you too can successfully transition from singleness to oneness as a married couple. This doesn't mean we live a frugal life. We travel, enjoy eating out and other pleasures, but we refuse to get caught up in overspending to the detriment of our marriage. Our household isn't filled with strife, anger, disagreement and frustration. We put God first in all that we do and allow Him to lead and guide our path in this world. We are encouraged by the psalmist that God will *"show us his ways and teach us his paths and guide us in his truth"* (Psalm 25:4-5).

changing your perception of your priorities can change your life in a powerful and meaningful way

So many people don't have such harmony in their relationships or households because they are living out of order. Proverbs 20:3 says, *"it is to a man's honor to avoid strife, but every fool is quick to quarrel."* I can assure you that changing your perception of your priorities can change your life in a powerful and meaningful way.

We are unable to achieve any of our goals unless we first decide in our minds that this is what we want to do and what God had in mind for us to do, for it is *"God who works in us both to will and to do His good pleasure"* (Philippians 2:13). You must begin to examine what you think, how you feel and what you believe or don't believe. No matter what, accepting these truths begins and ends with you.

Some of you may be control freaks who believe you must be in control of every facet of your life. You know who you are. Things on the job must be according to how you want it done; happiness may elude you at home unless your husband, wife, or child does everything according to your wishes. So many of us want to have complete control over our lives, yet the key to balance is discovering how you let go and let God have complete control over you. You see *"the mind controlled by the Spirit is life"* (Romans 8:5-6). You must turn your job, home, children, marriage, finances, and future, over to God and just enjoy the journey. When you do, I can assure you that peace and joy will be abundant in your life (John 10:10b).

It Begins With Remembering

In order to examine how you have come to know and understand what your priorities are, it's imperative to take personal stock as to who you are and how you got to your present point in life.

That mean's looking back at your life and how you were raised.

All of us don't come from homes where a relationship with God was firmly established; some people have never experienced loving parents or guardians who provided a proper and balanced outlook on life.

What we learned, saw and experienced greatly determines our view on marriage, job and relationships with friends. And in the absence of a personal relationship with God, many of us do not trust God, or ourselves because we believe that since we have experienced heartache and pain, surely God isn't present in our life (Psalm 53:1).

My view and experiences with my family allow me to enjoy a healthy adult life. We lived a life of family and love, and not one where my parents were never home because they worked 20 hours a day.

I had the pleasure of having my mother for a Sunday school

teacher and a father who chauffeured me around everyday. We were and have always been an extension of each other. Some would think being at church every Sunday would be a drag for a six-year old or embarrassing having your dad "the cabby" take you to school. That did not bother me. Honestly, I was happy not to ride the school bus.

Because of the life experiences afforded me, I was able to come in contact with people from different cultures, religions and family backgrounds. I had the opportunity to participate in tap, interpretive and modern jazz dance, gymnastics, as well as work as a youth volunteer at Houston's renowned M.D. Anderson Cancer Hospital.

I recognize how all of my experiences showed me that the younger you are exposed to life the more you can get out of it as time goes on. And the older I got the more I knew that I had been set apart for God's service with women, children and families.

While listening to today's' advocates for the poor, needy, and those who are slighted because of their color, economic status, or education; I am often compelled to help those in need. As young children we often see or hear stories of family members who worked as caregivers to other families, and each time they went to town they had to sit at the back of the bus, pick up their food from the rear door of a restaurant and listen to people call them names. The experiences of generations past, greatly impact our outlook and the work we choose on behalf of ourselves and others.

As I reflect on my early childhood, I fully understand why I do what I do and why I think how I think. I can recall visits to my great-grandmother's house on her acre and a-half lot. We picked pomegranates, small country peaches, and had our fill of her wisdom speeches. Was it the gumdrop tree on the center of the kitchen table, the high four-post bed and the three-step ladder used to get in it that makes me love my early childhood? The history and heritage told to us at family reunions taught me early to appreciate things that were different and to respect the city and country life. Just within my own family, I learned the importance of appropriateness and how people are treated differently because of their looks. I have been able to excel not in spite of, but because of my exposure. We must learn how to utilize all our life experiences.

The women in my family who served in ministry before me paved the way for who I am today. My great-grandmother was a godly woman who loved good preaching and simple entertainment, the likes of Oral Roberts, Billy Graham, and Lawrence Welk. I spent many days rehearsing their sermonic and instructional form to the chickens and goats. I had to make my own entertainment. Being the only child for eight years taught me how not to be a co-dependent adult.

> "We fail to remember how, why and what the Lord has done."

Delighting In The Lord

Of course, I had a little drama in my life growing up – who hasn't? And when we learn to take the good with the bad, we see the beauty of it all. It is when we fail to see the grace of God interwoven in our confusion that we begin to live with warped views about all aspects of life.

Yes, I am not happy about some of the things that have happened to me, but I fully understand that *"all things do work together for the good of those who love the Lord and are called according to His purpose"* (Romans 8:28).

Once when I had finished a seminar a young man approached me and wanted to know why every time he crossed one hurdle another would come soon after. As I think about this question even now, I still come back to the same answer, "We fail to remember how, why and what the Lord has done."

No sooner than we recover from one encounter we quickly jump into something else. We should all remember to look before we leap. Failing to take an accurate inventory of what we know or don't know will give the devil an opportunity to trick us in areas where we are already exposed and vulnerable (Ephesians 4:27).

Scripture records how the children of Israel had forgotten what the Lord had done for them. And in doing so they allowed their minds to be concerned with what was happening to them, thereby allowing the enemy to trick them, which made them forget the Lord was their redeemer. Psalm 78:42 says, *"They did not remember his power, the day He redeemed them from the oppressor, the day He displayed His miraculous signs in Egypt, His wonders in the region of Zoan."*

As the children of Israel faced impossible odds in the Desert and left Pharaoh's house, they encountered their own short-sightedness. They complained to Moses against the blessings of God and determined that they would have preferred to die in the palace oppressed than the desert free from oppression (Exodus 14:10-14). Oh, how the children of Israel had missed the big picture and so do we. If we are going to delight in the Lord, we must be able to see what we are facing and then brace ourselves for the journey ahead.

There are eight key truths that we can take away from Exodus 14:

- Recognize when you are facing impossibility.
- Mentally navigate through your impossibility.
- Take a positive outlook toward your impossibility.
- Understand your options in your impossibility.
- Discover the trouble with your impossibility.
- Respect the timing of your impossibility.
- Move beyond your impossibility.
- Give testimony about your impossibility.

As you read how the children of Israel escaped Pharaoh, take the time to study their journey and how they went on to fulfill their purpose in the land of opportunity.

You too will be inspired to take another look at your life and how it is governed. Are you harping on old things that have yet to be resolved? Have you forgotten what God has done for you? It seems that we only want to praise and give God glory when everything is going well. And maybe we can muster up enough gumption to give Him thanks or call on Him when we find ourselves in a bind or need another fix!

But God desires us to remember Him at all times. God has yet to be unfaithful to those who believe. Today, recall the benefits and blessings the Lord our God has displayed. Rejoice in the fact that we will always have victory because of Jesus' once and for all sacrifice. No matter how difficult things become, never forget the grace of God. His grace will never forget you.

when we are spiritually on point with God, something is bound to happen

Waiting On A Breakthrough

Are you waiting for a breakthrough? Does some situation have you held hostage and you are seemingly unable to break free? Maybe you are in an abusive situation or a dead end job and you cannot seem to find your way out. Hold on, help is on the way!

And then it happens. You lose your job or your mate leaves you, but you are unable to see the blessing in either because you are so caught up in your drama! And Lord knows there have been plenty of those days. It is then the rubber of your situation meets the road of your faith.

Rather than talking to God about what He has in mind, we spend time discussing with outsiders how such a thing could happen. We all at some time or another are caught in an array of bondages, so that once freed we see it as a burden rather than a blessing! *"God's ways are not our ways, His thoughts are not our thoughts"* (Isaiah 55:8), and our perception about God should now begin to match what He is saying about himself. Because when we are spiritually on point with God, something is bound to happen. You delight yourself in the Lord by reading His word daily and having scripture in your head and heart that will allow you to focus on what God is doing in your life. Your breakthrough is on the way once you put the word of God into practice. When you do you will see that receiving the desires of heart is closer than you think. (Psalm 37:4)

Have you considered being laid-off as God's way of giving you more time to spend with your kids or a way of escape to leave a job that was leading down a path with no chance for advancement? What about a troublesome relationship? Consider this as God's way of saying that man will no longer beat you and your children now have a chance for a brighter, more positive future. Or she is no longer able to poison the children's and your spirit with bitterness and lies. When we remember what could be, and see that all our situations have a silver lining, we can appreciate a need to change how we think about what happens to us.

A loss is sometimes a win. And a loss in your life could certainly be the breakthrough you need (Philippians 1:19-21). Remember, perception is based on how you view things. In some cases, your perception of what is bad can actually be good.

As I have grown older, I recall the things the Lord has done, such as how he saved me from a dog mauling at the age of two. I remember when he saved me from death by near drowning at age five. I can't forget how He rescued me from my abductors at the age of eleven. How he protected and healed me at age eighteen from date rape.

There is no doubt that given these issues or any other set of circumstances we would want to take matters in to our own hands. But is that the way of the Lord for us? I am grateful to have God first in my life so that my path is guided by Him.

I can't act like I've always been completely trusting. There have been times I tried to take matters into my own hands and quickly became frustrated. I soon realized that the path I had chosen for myself was not the path the Lord had mapped out for (Jeremiah 10:23; Proverbs 16:9). I have been like many others who have traveled on the road to another breakdown rather than a breakthrough. This is not uncommon. We get just a little break and we think we are ready to take on the world.

Sadly, once we are no longer bound we have a tendency to try to fill our own voids with what we think is best for us. And a vicious cycle continues to force us into the trap of seeing with our eyes and not the eyes of God. It was at this juncture that I surrendered my all to the Lord.

Filling your own voids is a sure sign when your spirit is not at rest and that you have gone too far with your own will. I recognize that we can become trapped and not even realize it. When working on filling a void in your life, here is a list of things to consider:

- **Don't drink in excess.** It will impair your reasoning. (Ephesians 5:18; Proverbs 23:21; Proverbs 23:25-29)

- **Don't overeat.** You won't have the strength you need to press on. (I Corinthians 8:7-8)

- **Keep your business to yourself.** Too many ideas will confuse you. (Proverbs 25:17)

- **No need to solve your problems via intoxicating substances.** You must become dependent on God and not pills. (Ephesians 5:15-17; Galatians 5:19-21)

- **Avoid temptations.** Spending money is not a proper outlet. All that does is create a problem with debt. The same goes for burying your troubles in the bedroom. A sexual addiction will also lead to other problems that may take longer to recover from than your original issue. (Proverbs 22:24-25; Ephesians 5:3)

- **Remain active in church.** If you are sick, do you avoid the doctor? No! Spirit-filled people will keep you in prayer, serve as wonderful prayer partners, and keep you spiritually grounded. (Hebrews 10:24-25)

- **Lose the bitterness.** Harboring ill-will towards someone will act as a cancer inside of your body. All it does is make you angrier and keeps you entrapped in your dilemma. The sooner you free your mind, body and spirit of hate and jealousy, the sooner God can instill peace, joy and happiness inside of you. (Proverbs 29:11; Galatians 5:22-26)

Make An Appointment With God

As we continue on this trek towards greater balance, we must make the effort to put God on our daily "things to do" list (Psalm 90:12). Palm Pilots, our Blackberry, Microsoft Outlook, and Franklin planner are the order of the day for many of us. We have become adept at scheduling everything in our life. I know of some married couples that schedule moments of intimacy. Now that's going a bit too far!

Making sure God is first and foremost on our schedule is crucial to achieving a balanced life. That is certainly the case when we are uncertain about issues in our life and we are trying to piece the puzzle together (Colossians 4:12).

That "me-time" with God is crucial because the still moments allow us to take inventory of our dilemma, and ourselves and allow God to speak to our minds and heart (Psalm 63:1-2).

In our home we have set aside a room specifically for prayer and meditation. It is a simple bedroom that we have converted as the space where we can get away from the TV, phone and even each other to spend time in the presence of the Lord.

Anyone who visits our home knows that if anyone of us in the room, we are not to be disturbed. Unless the house is on fire or there is an emergency we are not to be bothered.

This time alone puts us in the proper state of mind to listen to God's direction for us (Proverbs 19:21). The room can be used for bible study, reading of other spiritually based books or for times of reflection. If you don't have the opportunity to set aside a room for this purpose, choose a particular place in your home to serve as your own personal "altar." I have a church member who has chosen her closet as the get-away location. Again, the place could be large or small. The key is to have such a place to sit with God to hear His directives. Biblical history teaches that *"Jesus went up as usual"* to a place to find peace and commune with God (Luke 39:40-42; Matthew 26:36-39).

The time spent meditating and praying also plays a huge role in healing from our past wars. It is difficult to heal and hear God speak when you are constantly entangled (Hebrews 12:1-3). God says *"that if my people who are called by his name, will humble themselves and pray and seek my face, I will hear from heaven and heal their land"* (2 Chronicles 7:14). Do you want to be healed? Are you willing to change your perception of your life and God in order to live a life that is pleasing to Him? In order to do so, you must begin by letting some things in your life go.

Changing Your Perspective

Now that you are aware of how you think and what is happening to you, think about what it will take to acquire a 20/20 vision about your life from this moment on.

I understand how easy it is to lose focus of your goals and dreams. We get a job, lose jobs, voluntarily leave them, move from one relationship to another, get married and possibly have children. And before you know it you have not had a chance to finish school or take any of the professional opportunities afforded to you.

You have nothing to lose by exercising your right to do nothing!

The opposite is true for others. Some have taken every job opportunity and promotion offered and missed out on marriage and family. And, most importantly building a relationship with God.

To no avail, some things pass us by, never to be opened to us again. When you are trapped in unending cycles of misery, you are caught. Then the enemy ecstatically yells, "Gotcha!"

The key to clarity is learning to clear your mind. (2 Corinthians 3:17). And it starts with walking away from what your are facing at the moment. We always end up putting off the good stuff until we get through the crap. Just simply say, "Enough is enough!" We all have the same amount of time in life. There are 365 days a year; 52 weeks in a year; 30 days in a month; 12 months in a year; 24 hours in a day; 7 days in a week, 60 minutes in an hour, 60 seconds in a minute. How you manage your time will be the difference between balance and frustration.

Tomorrow morning get up, get dressed and do something for five minutes that relates to nothing on your list of things to do. Or get up, don't get dressed and do absolutely nothing but look out of the window, the door or stare at the ceiling. The idea is that you break your present cycle in order to expand your mind to the possibility of other things.

The amazing insight of this exercise is phenomenal. Acting as a responsible, free and independent believer gives way to explore the use of the gifts that God has endowed you. Even God rested on the seventh day (Genesis 2:2; Exodus 20:8). Are you not entitled to one day of rest and relaxation? You have nothing to lose by exercising your right to do nothing!

As you proceed on the Christian journey, allow God to show you the way. Put your hope and trust in Him and enjoy all that life has to offer. When you lean and depend on Him, you will find endless possibilities in your family life, career, ministry and personhood.

Our God is an awesome God and He will give you *"inexpressible and glorious joy"* (1 Peter 1:8). If you are seeking new directions in life, remember it begins with you. Rather than focusing and concentrating on any one or two things in particular, simply delight yourself in the Lord. God has always remained faithful to those who believe (2 Timothy 2:13). And at times when you forget his tender mercies and loving kindness, you will find that even then He will restore you over and over again.

Journaling: The Law Of Perception

There are some things that you will need to handle in order to get started with changing your perspective.

Turn to the "Journaling for Personal Growth" section of the book. As you begin to journal, be open and honest with yourself about what you are facing and feeling. You may find yourself uncertain about what you want to write. Take your time. When you are ready you will know exactly what to express and how to express it.

Meditative Moments

As you prepare for your time alone with God, take a few moments to quiet your mind, body and spirit. Turn now and read "Balanced Living Time" and let's get ready to hear God speak. Today's balanced living technique is Meditation for Mental Clarity. We will begin with a simple relaxation pose.

This is a pose of total relaxation where while lying on your back; you can either position yourself in the bed or on the floor. If you find any discomfort in your lower back or neck, place a rolled towel beneath your hips or neck for support. I find that as I wake each morning this position allows me to focus on my day before I get out of bed. While lying still I am able to pray to God for direction and guidance, and alleviate any overnight tension from a restless night of sleep. I simply wake with a few deep, calming breaths to thank God for allowing me to see another day.

Benefits:
- Calms the brain and helps relieve stress and mild depression
- Relaxes the body
- Reduces headache, fatigue, and insomnia
- Helps to lower blood pressure

Prayer Focus: Those who are unusually stressed.

Date: _____

Heavenly insight you have gained:

List a personal quality you are learning about yourself.

List two positive words of affirmation to speak into your life. Write what you anticipate to happen in your life from these words.

List the names of three people who you will encourage today. Purposely, seek them out in order to enrich their lives with your influence.

The Law of Promise

"… My word goes out from my mouth: it will not return to me empty, but will accomplish what I desire and achieve the purpose for which I sent it." Isaiah 55:11

A Promise Is A Promise

If God said it, then there is nothing more to be said. Once God has made his promise to us we are to understand that he will never fail us. We are now required to fully embrace his word and allow him to lead and guide us in everything that we do (Psalm 145:13).

When God makes a promise it is a covenant being made and one that will be kept. A covenant is defined biblically as a contract or agreement expressing God's gracious promises to His people and their consequent relationship to Him. We live in a world where we run to court for any little thing. But there is no need to seek a lawyer or mediator when God makes a covenant with us. His covenant is stronger than any earthly contract or bond in existence. (Matthew 16:19)

let's be honest; we sometimes have no idea how our situation will turn out.

In biblical history a covenant was brought about by God telling Abraham and other prophets and priests to cut up certain animals as a sacrifice to Him. In turn God would reveal himself and make a reality that which was shown to them. (Genesis 15). In this covenant the Lord would work through Abrams' willingness to sacrifice his son and suggest to us that God's covenant was unconditional and no matter what Abram did or did not do, God would honor His word. In scripture there are three kinds of covenants:

Between people. The covenant between friends, such as Jonathan and David is an alliance of love and loyalty (1 Samuel 18:1).

"After David had finished talking with Saul, Jonathan became one in spirit with David, and he loved him as himself" (I Samuel 18:3). *"And Jonathan made a covenant with David, because he loved him as himself"* (I Samuel 18:3, 20:8; 23:18).

Between God and man. This is the most important covenant of all because of an oath and promised blessings based on obedience and chastisement for disobedience. Consider the promise to the descendants of Moses that they would *"enter a land of milk and honey"* (Exodus 3:8), that was not fulfilled until the time of Joshua's rule (Joshua 1:1-9).

Covenants and the Bible. In the life of the believer, a promise or covenant is spoken in scripture and will yield what it represents to the one who puts it into practice in their life. For example: *"Delight yourself in the Lord and he will give you the desires of your heart"* (Psalm 37:11). This is what I call 'a prerequisite to a blessing'. It is where you have to do your part in order to see God's parts actualized. This is not contingent upon God, but upon each and every person who trusts in His word. You cannot get the desires of your heart if you do not put into practice the teachings of God. And yet it does not mean that God does not possess the ability to give those desires whether you do your part or not.

As a believer there is an understanding that whatever God has set in motion for you will be yours when you put your faith and trust in Him (2 Samuel 22:31). The Law of Promise is valid on the premise that a promise of God does not warrant scrutiny.

Have you heard a child say, "But you promised!" We have a tendency to think that when someone promises us something that they should not go back on their word. Yet, we know that with people, not all promises will become a reality. However, with God, a promise is a promise. A promise is to have positive connotations, not negative ones. What if I told you that there is no possibility for you to fail in any of the things you do today? Yes, you can be a complete success when what you are doing lines up with the will of God for your life and you are patterning your ambitions and accomplishments after his word. When God puts His word in motion, we are to follow it in order to reap what it has to offer (Psalm 119:160).

But when we are not doing everything God asks and we want to cover our emotions or wrong doing; we give out short terse answers when someone attempts to engage us in a conversation. When someone asks us how we are dong, our natural statement is, "fine." But let's be honest; we sometimes have no idea how our situation will turn out. And we know we are not fine. We just don't want to hash out our business right then and there. We are upset, angry and frustrated, and answer like "fine" is meant to move that person out of the way in a nice and easy manner. And no matter how many times we say it, it is empty and conceals our true needs and feelings. Keep this in mind the next time you use such a pat answer. You are either "Feeling Insecure, Neurotic and Emotional" or "Feeling Insecure, Needing Encouragement." In any event, something is not on point in your life.

When our lives are going haywire and we don't know what is going on, it's likely that this is what's happening. We rant, rave and act as if we are losing our mind over things that have little value whatsoever. When we say "fine" it is normally dripping with attitude or sarcasm. We are not being honest with others or ourselves, and the person we are talking to knows it as well. Such moments are filled with frustration that borders on the neurotic.

What we must learn to do is stay clear of non-essential encounters that lead us to act without thinking, which include:

- Having discussions about matters out of our control. (Proverbs 13:3)
- Listening to idle chatter about irrelevant stuff in your life. (John 8:47)
- Responding to ideas and concepts that aren't God's will. (I Corinthians 15:3)
- Making promises you can't keep. (Colossians 3:9-10)

In everything you do you should consider going with your first thought, which is often what God has placed in your spirit (John 14:26). But then we get in the way and want to begin to rationalize, justify and think of other scenarios, when God has already made clear and cleared a perfect path (Proverbs 16:9).

The law of promise offers the assurances that God will be near and available to your deepest need, no matter how large or small (Psalm 34:4). The word "near" is in the scriptures 331 times in the New International translation of the bible. It is indicative of the presence of God that is available at all times to those who are in need. Use the word of God to guide and keep you on a daily basis. Here are few "help is on the way" scriptures that can lead to your personal rescue. Go ahead! I dare you to use these scriptures and take God at his word to set your path straight from this moment on.

Help is on the way!

"Do not be far from me, for trouble is near and there is no one to help." Psalm 22:11

"Come near and rescue me; redeem me because of my foes." Psalm 69:18

"But as for me, my feet had almost slipped; I had nearly lost my foothold." Psalm 73:2

"But as for me, it is good to be near God. I have made the Sovereign Lord my refuge; I will tell of all your deeds." Psalm 73:28

"We give thanks to you, O God, we give thanks, for your Name is near; men tell of your wonderful deeds." Psalm 75:1

"Even the sparrow has found a home, and the swallow a nest for herself, where she may have her young; a place near your altar, O Lord Almighty, my King and my God." Psalm 84:3

"The Lord is near to all who call on him, to all who call on him in truth." Psalm 145:18

When was the last time you invited God to invade your comfort *do what God has promised he said he would for you. It is not God who torments you with your past, but the enemy*

zone? When did you accept an invitation from his word to draw closer to Him? I don't mean when you say, "I know God is over my life and I believe in Him." No, consider earnestly when you really and truly trusted God with everything. *Everything!*

There are always going to be times when we have doubts or are discouraged about what is happening in our life. Some of those include not communicating with our spouse for months, leading us to feel we are drifting apart; when the boss at work is working our last nerve, even though you are a dedicated employee; when your children have begun to act erratic and defiant, and we are hoping and praying that it's a phase. We do not want it to be peer pressure or a reliance on alcohol or drugs.

No one, and I mean no one, is immune to such doubt or discouragement. In 1 Samuel there were times when Samuel was distraught and discouraged and even doubted his own effectiveness. But his close circle of friends and family were there to encourage him during the difficult periods. Your are not alone in your despair; see the anguish of Samuel, Saul and David and how God offers His comfort.

- Lord said to Samuel, *"How long will you mourn for Saul, since I have rejected him as king over Israel? Fill your horn with oil and be on your way; I am sending you to Jesse of Bethlehem. I have chosen one of his sons to be king."* (1 Samuel 16:1)

- *"Now the Spirit of the Lord had departed from Saul; and an evil spirit from the Lord tormented him."* (1 Samuel 16:14)

- *"Whenever the spirit from God came upon Saul, David would take his harp and play. Then relief would come to Saul; he would feel better, and the evil spirit would leave him."* (1 Samuel 16:23)

- David said to Saul, *"Let no one lose heart on account of this Philistine; your servant will go and fight him."* (1 Samuel 17:32)

Not only do we need others to encourage us, we sometimes have to encourage ourselves. David, Saul's son, had to do this very thing as he was being chased and mocked by his own father: *"When those who were carrying the ark of the Lord had taken six steps, he sacrificed a bull and a fatten calf. David, wearing a linen ephod, danced before the Lord with all his might, while he and the entire house of Israel brought up the ark of the Lord with shouts and the sound of trumpets"* (2 Samuel 6:13-15).

What we cannot forget is that doubt acts as a poison to the Spirit. It robs us of the joy and gratitude that so easily or naturally comes from being a child of God (Psalm 42:11). God reminds us *"that perfect love casts out fear"* (I John 4:18). So there are going to be days of dismay, but we will prevail.

Discouragement is an equally dangerous emotion, which often stems from faulty beliefs, misconceived ideas, lies from past experiences or lack of closure to unfortunate encounters. All of this can be extremely volatile when we have built our lives on any one of them.

In some of the most adversarial periods of our life, we learn to muster up the encouragement to make it through the indecisive times.

In short, it distracts you from receiving the fullness of God's promises. And if you don't overcome those doubts and bouts of discouragement, you may be crippled and unable to do what God has promised he said he would through you. It is not God who torments you with your past, but the enemy. For God *"will forgive our wickedness and will remember our sins no more"* (Hebrews 8:12).

Accepting God's Invitation

When struggling with doubt and discouragement, we can't lean to our own understanding (Proverbs 3:5). We shouldn't call every friend, text it, Twitter it, Blog about it, place it on Facebook, or Fark it, all hoping someone will provide the magical word to cure your ailment. And I surely do not believe in wasting money, time and resources in Tarot card readings to decide ones fate or as if a medium can speak to your situation.

It is God's Word and God's Word alone that can get you beyond the doubt and discouragement and unlock the many mysteries of His promises. We have to always remember that trouble will come our way (Romans 10:12-13). We must remain on our knees in prayer and completely trust in Him. James records *"that in this life you will have trials and tribulations, yet count it all joy"* (James 1:2-5).

Read that again. It says, *"... in this life you will have trials and tribulations, yet count all joy."* James says we will have difficulties in life, yet in the midst of your pain and suffering, we can count it all joy because the protection God gives is available to us as we encounter the trials of life.

The book of Isaiah offers an invitation to those who desire to discontinue living an empty life and who seek to recover from past discouragement, doubt and indecision. Read Isaiah 55:1-13 and we will discover together nine keys to recovery.

Carefully read each line and pray that God will reveal to you how He will enrich and enhance your life. Is your life out of control? Trust God to put it in order.

Isaiah's Nine Keys To Recovery:

1. God gives us an open invitation. (Verse 1)
2. Only God can completely satisfy our needs. (Verse 2)
3. The invitation is to all who want what God has to offer. (Verses 3-5)
4. God warns that he may not always be as close as he is at this very moment. (Verse 6)
5. Only God will grant forgiveness for anything you have done. (Verse 7)
6. God tells us we cannot presume to know how to repair ourselves. (Verses 8-9)
7. God plans and prepares a harvest to those who will receive Him. (Verses 10-11)
8. Only God can give you the peace and joy you need to sustain you. (Verse 12)
9. God wants to leave a legacy in this life through you. (Verse 13)

Could it be that you have turned your life over to your friends, family, career or inward toward self? Without your life placed in the Master's hands the enemy will continue to deceive you and rob you of the joy that God desires to give.

God is so much greater than we are. You can trust Him though you do not understand everything that happens.

To truly benefit from the Law of Promise, God allows you to set aside your fears and embrace his loving power by accepting and believing his word. *"Who is it that overcomes the world? Only he or she who believes that Jesus is the Son of God"* (I John 5:5). Do you want to overcome the problems that are plaguing you? Then set your hope fully on the grace of God to be given to you when you surrender yourself to Him. You don't have to spend money going to counseling or taking medication to regulate your blood pressure or stress levels. You simply have to believe that God can handle your situations.

You already know that the enemy will attack when we are vulnerable and at the most inopportune times. He attacks you when you are sick. He attacks when you are low on self-esteem. He attacks when you are down on your luck. He attacks when your bills are out of control, all adding to your feelings of inadequacy and failure. But God is ready to deliver you!

To be an overcomer, here are three helpful tips. First, acknowledge that the situation is out of your hands. Secondly, believe that God will help you when ask for it with gratitude. Finally, concentrate on what you can control. Discover the joy of dismissing the idea that your life would be better if someone else has done something else. However true that statement may be, you personally can do something differently to turn it all around. Think about something in your life that you need to overcome and ask the Lord to help you.

The law of promise is available to you because God is a covenant keeping God and that whatever he puts in motion will not come back without completing its assignment.

Each of the nine steps to recovery in Isaiah 55 causes you to take an inventory of your life and find out where you may have faced major hurdles that seemed impassable at the time. Some of our problems, let downs and sad occurrences in life lead us to see clearly the path that God is mapping out. Many of our burdens are to build us up and not to keep us down (James 1:4; 12).

It's Not Just A Phase

There are a few times in life that require a closer look to see how they impact us. We have a tendency to say that we are going through a phase, but in actuality God is working His best work as we mature or are going through adversity (Psalm 119:9-16). Let's take a closer look together at pivotal points that may have or can define us in a lifetime.

- ✓ *Evaluating your childhood.* How do your experiences with your family measure up to how you would raise your own children?

- ✓ *Evaluating your teen years.* What was the most memorable event in your teenage life? How has it shaped you as a person?

- ✓ *Developing life skills in your 20's.* Are you ready for adulthood? What significantly caught you off guard in this ten-year period?

- ✓ *Redefining your life skills in your 30's.* What are you learning from your mistakes? How are you coping with your decisions?

- ✓ *Accepting reality in your 40's.* Some things in life are not meant to be. No matter how hard you tried to turn things around, you were not quick enough to stop the outcome that has become a lifelong challenge.

- ✓ *Embracing freedom past your 50's.* You are at the empty nest stage or close to it. You are ready to travel or at least do not have to be home to take care of anybody!

- ✓ *Learning to give unconditionally.* Your time is your own and you can give it away freely. You can volunteer at the shelter, become a mentor, life coach, stay home and rest, or simply send a donation to your favorite charity.

- ✓ *Coping with the unexpected.* Hey, admit it. You knew the grand-kids would be coming to stay sooner or later. Life has dealt harshly with your own children and they need your help. Again!

- ✓ *Acquiring the skills of resilience.* It's tough being the strong one, but you know exactly why God has blessed you... so you can bless others. You endure it all very gracefully.

- ✓ *Loving yourself and others in the midst of it all.* No matter what happens you are there for your family. And when you think about it, you would not have done a single thing differently.

Scripture reveals that we are not to worry about the small things in life, but to focus on what we can control (Matthew 6:25-33).

God relates to his people with unconditional provisions. He takes care of our food, shelter, and clothing. He even gives us cognitive ability, talents and gifts to cultivate skills so we can earn a living (Deuteronomy 7:12-26; 8:18). We in return are to have a sacrificial lifestyle and unwavering faith toward God. God does not ask much from us. We are to read his word, live by it and share it with others. Life is really that simple. We make it harder. Do we shun God out of fear? Ignorance? Defiance?

The Law of Promise assures us we will not find ourselves deceived again by misplaced trust, *"rather, we have renounced secret and shameful ways; we do not use deception, nor do we distort the word of God. On the contrary, by setting forth the truth plainly we commend ourselves to every man's conscience in the sight of God"* (2 Corinthians 4:2). The promises people make to us cannot always be kept because they do not possess the authority to make them realities. And with our "pipe dreams" and desire to live another's version of the American dream, we fall hook, line and sinker for the bait. We must learn to live in a positive manner our own reality; whether poor, middle-class, or wealthy. We can have our version of the dream and be at peace with the blessing.

When we act upon the words of what has deceived us, we find that we have been lied to and tricked. And what hurts the most is that we have built our lives on falsehoods; those activities in life that we have participated in that were done because of false information. Consider the person who is sold a bill of goods and decides to invest in the project. Years go by and they have built homes, lifestyles, made other investments and then one day they find out it's a scam. All of their hopes, dreams and way of living have just dissipated right before their eyes. Many people get caught in such schemes. Not only does this happen to us professionally, it happens personally. Here are other areas that we find ourselves caught-up in based on "half-truths" as well:

Relationships. Most of our pain and suffering is over broken relationships. Whether you are married, single, separated, widowed or divorced the agony of disappointment exists for those who are experiencing the emotional and sometimes physical loss.

Finances. Whether too much or too little, money can put stress on us. Because we do not possess the financial savvy to balance family needs and the continuous rise in the cost of living, we often find ourselves strapped for cash and unable to make ends meet.

Social adjustments. Moving to a new city or school can cause emotional upheaval. Learning how to fit in and deal appropriately with the unfamiliar can cause us to lose a sense of balance and perspective. Having the added pressure of dealing with newness can weigh heavily on us.

Spiritual maturity. Whether you are a mature or recent believer, you will find your share of heartbreaking moments. As you grow in your faith you will discover that not everything you want to do will come when you want it. You will have to learn the art of patience, persistence and prayer for your survival in the kingdom of God.

Work issues. Dealing with difficult people can get your juices flowing. In a work environment we do not have a say about who works with us or who takes lunch and breaks with us, or shares a cubicle with us. Work can be taxing. There are many personality types around us all day long.

Family concerns. In our society of too little time, more and more people are opting out of the workplace in order to spend more time with family. Mothers and fathers are looking for more ways to spend quality time with each other and their children.

Emotional baggage. Whatever your problem, it is clearly recognizable to everyone. You wear your emotions on your sleeve, you have outbursts, you get irritated easily or you just simply opt out of the game of life altogether. Your baggage is weighing you down and it is time to release it by sorting out what you are carrying around. Sometimes you have to do it piece by piece, looking at every aspect of what you are carrying and assessing its value and if it will ever have value in your life again.

Selfishness. "It's not all about you!" The phrase my mother used was "the world does not revolve around you little girl!" I learned quickly by having things constantly change around me. That made me realize that I was not the center of attention and nor had God intended it to be that way. It is all about God and what He has given us in order to give back to others.

Other. _____. Express yourself. I am sure you can add a few of your own life learning experiences.

Your life is on the verge of being tremendously blessed. When you measure all your failings against the unconditional love of God and His authority to give you what you need when you need it, there is no stopping the flow of his spirit in your life.

In order for this principle to be a reality, you must:

1. *Accept* God at His word. (James 1:21)
2. Realize you are a *chosen vessel.* (1 Peter 2:9)
3. Believe God will not be *unfaithful* to Himself or you. (2 Timothy 2:13; 2 Samuel 22:26, 27)

So what do you think? Are you ready to take God and His word at face value? As you allow yourself to embrace these keys to balance your outlook on life, get ready to see some real changes. I am personally able to keep my word by not making empty promises because I have been given a model to live by. And not only do I trust that God will provide ample opportunities for me, but that He will only send those opportunities that are tailored for my life. I know that there is no failure in God and therefore when I do what God has set up for me, I too, will not be a failure!

Journaling: The Law of Promise

As you prepare for your writing and time of quiet reflection, pray and ask God to reveal to you people in your life that can benefit from the principles you are learning. There are people who are frustrated and upset about how things in their life are going. You now have an opportunity to share words of support, comfort and encouragement from God and His word.

Meditative Moments

Getting ready for your time of reflection can sometimes seem impossible when your mind is racing from the day's activity. For just a few moments prepare yourself with today's balanced living technique of meditation for quieting your nerves; a seated forward bend. Do not try this pose if you have a back injury.

When we are nervous about putting something new into practice, we may get an upset stomach or have trouble with digestion. This will also help when you are about to have a panic attack or severe chest pains. Our technique today will relax your body and mind.

Sit on the floor with your back to a wall to provide support or sit in a chair. You may also use a folded blanket to support your back and to lift your hips.

Once in an upright position, when you are ready, inhale and then exhale. On your third exhalation, slowly lean the body forward toward your knees. If you are unable to reach your knees with your head, modify your posture by reaching forward with your arms toward your toes or bending the knees slightly to alleviate pressure from the lower back. As you reach continue to clear your mind through breathing as you relax your back, stomach and hips.

Benefits:

- Calms the brain and helps relieve stress and mild depression
- Stimulates the liver, kidneys, ovaries, and uterus
- Improves digestion
- Helps relieve the symptoms of menopause and menstrual discomfort
- Soothes headache and anxiety and reduces fatigue
- Reduces high blood pressure and aids with infertility, insomnia, and sinusitis

my soul longs to worship, a God who truly satisfies

Prayer focus: Those in need of a positive outlook.

Date: _____

Heavenly insight you have gained:

List a personal quality you are learning about yourself.

List two positive words of affirmation to speak into your life. Write what you anticipate to happen in your life from these words.

List the names of three people who you will encourage today. Purposely seek them out in order to enrich their lives with your influence.

The Law of Thanksgiving

"...Ascribe to the Lord the glory due his name.
Bring an offering and come before Him,
worship the Lord in the splendor of his holiness."
1 Chronicles 16:29

In All Things Give Thanks

I have discovered that to give thanks in all things requires me to praise Him everyday for everything (I Thessalonians 5:16-18). I accept that waiting until Sunday morning just might be too late! Why would I wait to express later how I am feeling right now? My praise is about appreciating God for what He has done, while at the same time my worship is about adoring God for who he is. And as a daily benefit and blessing to my life the two culminate at the apex of my love for God. There are times when I just cannot keep from waving my hands or tapping my foot or shouting Amen. And I may do it any moment during the week as the Spirit moves me.

I came to terms with the fact that my time of official worship does not have to be on any given Sunday, but is an everyday occurrence. Because more than when official worship should begin, the focus in our lives is where, and where is in the heart of the faithful who adore God not in spite of, but because of. The psalmist records, *"I will bless the Lord at all times, His praise will continually be in my mouth"* (Psalm 34:1). Because of His grace, tender mercies, loving kindness, patience, support, belief in me, daily favor, ever-lasting love, mighty acts, wisdom and host of other attributes, my soul longs to worship, a God who truly satisfies (Psalm 103:3-5).

Such worship reminds me of a cool glass of lemonade on a hot summer day. How quickly do I forget my parched throat? The same goes for worship when I am feeling the stresses of life. I am fulfilled by a worshipful countenance. Read Psalm 42:1-5 and notice how our souls are searching for fulfillment.

What a tribute to God as our heart seeks to be nourished and nurtured by an all-powerful God. At the depth of our despair and brokenness when all of life overwhelms us, our God is to the rescue to ease our pain and calm our fears. For it is not until we relinquish our control over our lives and totally surrender to God, that we can be honest with ourselves and be released from doubt and denial (John 8:32).

As you reflect over your life, consider these critical questions that arise from Psalm 42 to ascertain how you can begin to worship God *"in spirit and in truth"* (John 4:24).

Does your soul long for God? (V2) Think about what is happening in your life that causes you to want to seek God in such an earnest manner. Is there a void in your life that has separated you from the Lord? Recall in His word *"that nothing can separate you from the love of God."* (Romans 8:35-39). No matter how stressed or worried you become, God is right there with you.

What is taking you so long Lord to give me peace? (V3) People have a tendency to be mean and cruel when they inquire about how we are getting along in our situation. They raise the question, "Where is your God" more out of insult than true concern for what we are facing. You must realize that as your soul is being refreshed and revived, you will come under attack from those who do not understand how God works.

"Are you doing what you do to get credit from others?"

What happened to cause me to be out of touch with God?
(V4) We can get off focus very quickly in life. Our priorities change. Our life gets turned upside down. And before you

know it, we are no longer participating in things of God anymore or the things that brought us joy. How much did you "used to do?" Remember the passion and fire you carried for the things of God? You kept a joyful attitude about being a child of the King! Remember how excited you were about being a child of the King! Remember how excited you were about being a Christian no matter what happened? We should remember that place and seek to return there.

Will I ever find comfort again? (V5) There is no denying that life can deal harshly with us. And when we are in "desert moments" our souls get spiritually dry. *"Why are you downcast O my soul? Why so disturbed within me?"* the Psalmist asks. Consider that every time you deny God praise and worship, you are taking away from your own refreshment and time of spiritual revival.

But don't worry, there is hope. As you pray and meditate about your life and the missing pieces that only abiding in the presence of God can complete, you will be able to *"put your hope in God, for you will praise him, your Savior and your God."* (V11). Do you not know by now that your friends cannot help you when your soul is in despair? Unless you have already had a little talk with Jesus, no one can speak to your situation! You have to accept that all of your help comes from the Lord and then and only then will the Holy Spirit lead you to others, if needed, who can help walk you through the rest of the journey (Psalm 46:1).

All To Him I Owe

The Law of Thanksgiving causes us to re-think how we relate to God, others and ourselves. Our constant ability to take God for granted hinders our capability of seeing the positives knitted into our day (Romans 8:28).

Too often we believe that people owe us something because of our environment, history, ethnicity, class or creed, when in fact, we owe everything to God. Who we are and what we do is an extension of who God is (1 John 1:2-4).

The gifts, talents and skills we possess are driven by our desire to honor God for giving us new life (Ephesians 4:1-32). And even those who question the existence of God and who have sought to remove prayer and other forms of public displays are caused to fall in humble adoration because of His grace and mercies that are magnificently displayed through the most adversarial times in history.

I can honestly say that I have not had a problem with God. I can say this because for every time that God has chastised me or helped see things His way, I deserved it. I was either disobedient or just plain stubborn. I may not have liked the rebuke, but I was out of line and had it coming.

I recall when God wanted me to go to the hospital and pray over a woman who was very ill. He wanted me to take the anointing oil and dab it on the areas that He would reveal to me when I got to the hospital. I thought I knew better than God and said to the Lord, "if she would take better care of her body and do the regime prescribed for her, she would get well. Why must I go across town every month and deal with someone who is stubborn and refuses to be healed?" Oh my, did God ever get on me about my gift of healing and who was I to question how He wanted to use it! I now have a good understanding about my gifts and my response when he makes a biblical request (2 Timothy 3:16).

On the other hand, I know people who are continually unhappy. They are upset with God. They dislike people with whom they work. They are bitter and unappreciative of the opportunities that come their way. Whether the opportunity is serving God or others.

They constantly paint a sad picture and their outlook on life is bleak. The word says, *"that each heart knows its own bitterness, and no one else can share its joy"* (Proverbs 14:10). But wouldn't you agree that even when things are not at their best, you know they could be worse?

How many times in the course of the week do you come across people who have an odd disposition? There is always a person at work, church or in your family who is mean, miserable and mad about life. Is there not one good thing that happened to them that could turn their attitude toward life around?

Giving Credit Where Credit Is Due

Maybe the person needed a kind word or a "thank you" (Proverbs 12:25). In the world today the distribution of accolades for our efforts is often times ignored. And rarely, if ever, are kind words spoken about our performance at home, school, and church or on the job. It is here that our system of unconditional love and effort waiver, and we get emotionally caught up in being slighted rather than praising God for ourselves (Proverbs 15:13). Could this be another reason "why our soul becomes downcast and disturbed?" Are we looking too much to others to give us validation?

Giving God his props is an honorable thing to do

And yet the question remains that only you can answer: "Are

you doing what you do to get credit from others?" How many of you are waiting to receive the employee of the month award? Are waiting for the church to host a banquet in your honor? Or better still, waiting for your family to give you the "Family Member of the Year" award?

I believe there is a time and place to give credit to others and yes, definitely thanking God for giving us the ability to get the credit.

Each of us should strive to follow the example set out in 2 Thessalonians 1:3, *"We ought to always thank God for you, brothers, and rightly so, because your faith is growing more and more, and the love every one of you has for each other is increasing."*

I must admit that I am not always diligent in giving people credit when they deserve it. I get busy and caught up in my own work and deadlines and I fail to recognize the contributions others have made. I am grateful for the countless number of volunteers who give selflessly to projects I work on. Have you had people working so closely beside you on something that you took their presence for granted? As if they are just supposed to help you out!

While watching the movie *What Women Want,* a young woman in the film who was depressed and suicidal caught my attention. Each day as she passed out files, ran errands and handled the business of the office, her efforts went unnoticed, and her awareness of being under appreciated was showing (Proverbs 15:23). No one seemed to care that her work was piling up or that she did not feel as if she was apart of the team.

Many of us have felt that way or been the one to ignore another person. Today, encourage someone who has gone above and beyond the call of duty on your behalf; the secretary who gets you your messages and handles your personal errands; the cleaning lady who empties your trash at the end of the day; or your spouse, child or sibling who does their chores even if you had to ask them a thousand times. Come on now, don't get an attitude. Of course, it is their responsibility or in their job description, but a few kind words of job well done shows gratitude and appreciation; not for doing what they were hired or expected to do, but doing it with a certain style and care. Sometimes we just have to appreciate people for showing up. It says a lot about a person who shows pride and dignity in themselves and the work ethic.

So Much To Be Thankful For

When we consider the qualities and attributes of God's character, we come to fully appreciate it all. And yet we don't fully comprehend the magnitude of our God!

In America there is a self-made or pull-yourself-up-by-the-boot-straps mentality. They are always the folks who say that you shouldn't depend on someone else for help and that if you just work harder, your situation will improve. They say, "Forget talking about your problem," or "Just keep pushing and pushing and it will all work itself out."

But they are fooling themselves (Proverbs 12:8). People with this kind of philosophy find themselves distraught when they can't control, or get a grip on the momentum of negativity in their life. And yes, even these individuals who espouse their independent rhetoric are sometimes forced to look to others for help.

It is in these times of testing that you come to know the real you and appreciate your loved ones. Rather than focusing on the material, a shift is made toward the irreplaceable! As we grow in our faith we discover that experiencing the joy of God is an everyday occurrence.

We should not wait until the holidays or time of tragedy to realize the value of the people near and dear to us.

When I read the Psalms I am able to see that God takes care of our social, emotional, physical and spiritual needs (Psalm 147). He strengthens me when my family bond is severed at a funeral or when someone is in the hospital. When I see family members, I think about the times I put off calling a loved one or didn't go and visit grandma or grandpa or an aunt, sibling, or very dear friend when we had the chance. More than when we desire food on the table, clothes on our backs and requesting to be kept in our right mind, do we experience the benevolence of God in the midst of true hardship.

Other scriptures affirm that the righteous are not forsaken and never go around begging for anything (Psalm 37:25). Do you have health? Strength? Comfort? Joy? Peace? Here is when the words of Paul are clearer than ever, *"Rejoice in the Lard always, I say it again: Rejoice!"* (Philippians 4:4). We are to learn to look at inner well being as priceless in comparison to the value of material possessions.

Think for a moment. Does God know that you are sincerely grateful for His presence in your life? If you have not given *"God the glory due his name"* as spoken of in I Chronicles 16:28-29, then consider where you would be right now if the Lord had not stepped into your circumstance.

David in all his wisdom and misguided deeds had the sense to praise the Lord for restoring him to wholeness (1 Chronicles 16:8-11). All throughout this Praise of Thanksgiving that David has written, he continues to admonish the readers "to remember." Are you remembering the loving kindness that God has shown you?

Are you remembering that this time last year your future was uncertain? Are you remembering the heartache you experienced at the loss of a loved one, and how the Lord gave you joy and peace beyond measure?

Giving God his props is an honorable thing to do. It is the Lord who has built you up and has kept you when you were mistreated without cause and against your will. It is God who controls your situation and has a personal interest in its outcome. It is God who keeps you steady and balanced when the waves of life are tossing you here and there. It is God who continues to do what He does, because He is God! At this season in your life, rejoice. You have so much to be thankful for. *"Praise the Lord. How good it is to sing praises to our God, how pleasant and fitting to praise Him!"* (Psalm 147:1).

As I think about the goodness of the Lord, I cannot help but thank Him for who he is. All too often we thank God for the things that He has given us and fail to thank Him for just being God.

Praising God is testimony of his goodness – not ours – and we are reminded that God is in control and is looking out for us. God goes through our trials and tribulations with us and has allowed his son to suffer death to bring us to a place of pardon and forgiveness. Yes. First he pardons us then he forgives. He doesn't wait until we provide an explanation or apologize. Nor does He require us to jump through hoops. It is for this reason that our praise and adoration for God should fully honor Him.

It is in our worship to God that we are able to show our gratitude.

The provisions of God and the protection of God are made available to us because He loves us, no more, no less.

God is...to name a few!

Able	Gracious	Strong
Has Authority	Abounding in love	Supreme
Almighty	Has Integrity	Sure
Healing	All-knowing	Tender
All-powerful	Holy	True
Indescribable	Always Present	Understanding
Attentive	Invisible	Unfailing
Jealous	Awesome	Unconditional
Beautiful	Just	Unique
Kind	Blameless	Wise
Blessed	Last	Wonderful
Light	Compassionate	Loving
Worthy	Consuming Fire	*List other attributes:*
Enthroned	Majestic	
Eternal	Merciful	
Ever-present	Mighty	
Exalted	Patient	
Faithful	Perfect	
First	Protective	
Flawless	Pure	
Forgiving	Radiant	
Gentle	Righteous	

Finding Your Own Encouragement

By now you know that God works best when you cease to take matters into your own hands. But you may have feelings of guilt, doubt and shame that have caused you to harbor resentment toward yourself and others. You are not alone. One of the biggest lies and schemes of the enemy is to try and tell you that you are not forgiven. That is an absolute lie! The word of God reveals that not only does He *"cast out our sins as far away as the east is from the west"*

(Psalm 103:12), they are forgiven and forgotten (Isaiah 6:7).

When you find that your past is haunting you it is the devil, not God. You may be encouraged by these words and begin to realize how your life was spared when caught in adultery or how your heart was mended by hearing from an old friend, and rather than being broken to pieces over a relationship coming to an end, you were rather overjoyed by it. When we fail to capture the moments of surprise in our everyday routines we neglect the presence of the Lord in our life.

You see, I don't mind being transparent about my upbringing. I know why things were done the way they were and rather than being bitter about them, I accept that we had the best that was available to us at the time. In many classes of society "barely making it" is a way of life. And the sooner you accept it, the less heavy your heart will be about thinking you missed out on something all these years. You didn't.

Our experiences and encounters with God provoke and invoke us to share his goodness in ways we would have refused many years ago. We testify in song, writing and prayers about the blessings God has bestowed on us (Psalm 89:1; Psalm 101:1).

Several years ago, while teaching a discipleship class, a man exclaimed, "People ought to tell their story. When they do, others are blessed by it and God is glorified through it!" How right he is. When we tell what God is doing in our lives or how he delivered us from a sticky situation, others find out that they are not alone in their circumstances. To find our own joy you must learn to appreciate every aspect of your life. Yes, there are days when nothing is going your way, but just the fact you have a day to experience should cause you to sing until you are hoarse.

After September 11, 2001, my attitude toward deadlines, other people's attitudes and other trifling matters just drifted into oblivion. I simply refuse to let anyone or anything steal my joy!

You have got bragging rights. Whatever way today you want to let people know who God is to you, show it. Put post-it notes on your cubicle. Change your screen saver to a scripture quote. Visit a local center for the aging. Feed the homeless. Share your experiences about God with someone who may be seeking God.

Appreciating God through Worship

In our society there are many ways to show expressions of thanksgiving and appreciation to people we know. Cards, e-mail, flowers, text messages, pod-casts, video-casts, faxes, phone calls, love notes or gifts are just a few. Some may see these things as impersonal, however, it is true that "it's the thought that counts." And though these work for us, can you send any of these to God for all He has done and will do for you?

God knows that we cannot appreciate Him in the same manner that we do each other. In all His infinite wisdom, God provides us with the way in which we can express our thanksgiving to Him. It is in our worship to God that we are able to show our gratitude.

The biblical definition of worship is reverence, honor, praise and service shown to God. In both the Old and New Testaments, like much of life today, worship is misguided and misdirected to idols, people, false gods and images. Not all the crosses around our necks, the stained glass windows in churches or even the WWJD t-shirts can clarify as directly our love for God as bowing down and worshiping him. It is tragic that many worship gods they can carry, rather than place their trust fully on the God that can carry them.

In our quest for fulfillment, we realize how important it is to have a lifestyle of worship. It is more than singing songs and clapping our hands. It is an attitude that embodies all the characteristics of a Holy God. As believers we search for and long for a living God, even if and when our situations seem dead and lifeless. The word of God speaks of the Law of Thanksgiving, which is displayed for us by these three elements of true worship:

1. *My undivided attention is required when I worship*
2. *My participation is expected as I worship, and*
3. *My allegiance is demanded to the One I worship*

Our worship experiences have been tainted by traditionalism. People become embarrassed to raise their hands to praise God and give a wave offering. Others get funny looks when they stand to affirm the words of the choir or pastoral message. Some are even asked by other congregants to not return if they have displayed emotion in the Sunday service.

We have become too quiet at a time when the Lord says we can shout, sing, play instruments, dance around, clap our hands and generally have a party with and for the Lord. Consider Psalm 150 when we are encouraged to *"praise him with the sounding of the trumpet, praise him with the harp and lyre, praise him with the tambourine and dancing, praise him with the resounding cymbals."* The entire book of Psalms is a praise party.

While reading Psalm 95, I identified five key actions God makes available to us to become living instruments of praise and thanksgiving:

1. **Allow yourself to be in God's presence** (verses 1-2).
   God wants us to abide with him and use our voice to let
   others know that we have had a real encounter with Him
   and that we are the better for it.

2. **He has summoned us to worship** (verses 3-5). Our
   God is great, and contrary to popular opinion, is the king
   above all because He created the earth and it is His. There
   is no denying that God is all-powerful and warrants our
   attention.

3. **Recognize God working in us** (verses 6-7). In an effort
   to be truly reverent to God we are to bow down as a sign
   of surrender of our will to His. It is in this surrendering
   that we take on what He requires from us. Not only do we
   bow in reverence, we bow for our sins as a sign of lament
   for causing God pain in our disobedience. As we see the
   hand of God restoring us in our brokenness we become
   grateful to a heavenly Father who would bless His
   children in spite of their shortcomings.

4. **Stay a dedicated and committed believer** (verses 8-9).
   It will not be easy, but we need to learn dedication. In our
   dedication to the cause of Christ and our commitment to

serve faithfully, God reveals the purpose for our actions and attitudes. It will not be in vain that we suffer sometimes, but that in our pain we recognize the grace and mercy of God. And that no sooner than we think we can no longer stand it, God rewards us for our faithfulness and humility.

5. **Alienating God has consequences** (verses 10-11). To be willful and defiant causes the wrath of God to come upon us. For every action there is a consequence and as we mature in our faith we must accept the chastisement of God or suffer an even greater penalty – separation from the safety and provision of God.

Finding balance for your life is about finding balance with God. Not only does scripture teach us how and why we worship, it teaches us how to have honor and integrity in our day-to-day battles.

The truths of His words are everlasting and can have a profound effect on our lives when put into practice. Whether you are at home, work or church there should be a feeling of thanksgiving about God. Just because we are having a bad day or something did not go our way does not mean that God was absent from the situation. It may mean that God had something else in mind; something greater than we could ask, think or imagine.

It's All About God

Whether your glass is half empty or half full is not really the issue. Being thankful that you have a glass means you are grateful to have something to fill. It is important to seek out scriptures that challenge us to take action. We are to keep building on the firm foundation of Christ.

I admit there are times it seems impossible to go on. As I reflect on my early childhood, I have come to realize how blessed I am. By the age of five, I had three near death experiences. By my own estimation I should not be here. God has a plan and purpose for my life, one of which He knew He could trust me with. He would have not given me a chance to live if he did not believe that even in my straying, He could rely on me to be a vessel, He could use.

Read Psalm 139 to acquaint yourself with what God knows about you. He reveals a great plan He has for you and when it was planned. The enemy must have seen the record books before the foundation of the world about God's plan for me. He wanted to take me out before I ever had a chance to begin.

My life today still meets the unexplainable. However, I am readily aware of how and when the enemy is seeking to cause me to stumble and fall. But Jesus' promise is that He had come to give me life; life to the full of my desiring (John 10:10b).

Attaining the Law of Thanksgiving

I have been able to overcome my adversities because I let God take me to another level in my belief system. I learned to lean, trust and obey. The single most important act of worship for the Christian is the unqualified presentation of self to God as an obedient servant. This dedication involves all of you. You must learn to surrender your mind so that God can fill it with His wisdom and remove any doubt and misconceptions that could linger like residue and further clutter your life. Once you have surrendered your mind you must surrender your body.

You surrender your body because it contains the tools by which God's will is carried out. Our bodies are easily entangled in the mess of the world and yet it is the single most used instrument for fulfilling the promises of God.

When we devote ourselves to God, we become His instruments of praise by which He can impact the world. Such faithful and joyous worship makes our lifetime a blessed affair.

Here are three keys to get to the next level of your journey for a fulfilling life:

Accepting God's Will

I must have an expectation of a positive outcome.

There must be an implementation of a positive plan.

There is to be jubilation for what has been and is going to be accomplished.

These keys will give you an opportunity to realize the privilege of being a person with a thankful heart and an attitude of gratitude. Embracing the presence of God will help you rejoice even when things are not looking there best.

Thanksgiving is more than a few words or the shake of a hand. It is a way of life. As you reflect over the dangers seen and unseen in your life, will you thank God for His saving grace? Will you embrace Him? Will you allow Him to fill your life with joy? God is waiting for you. Receive Him today.

Journaling: The Law of Thanksgiving

Reflect quietly over your life and ask the Lord to reveal to you how much you have to be thankful for. There are times when we all had experiences knock us off our feet. However, we got up ready for the next round. Other experiences we have blocked out because we believe if we discussed them or thought about them they would destroy us emotionally.

Today, allow yourself to think about how and what the Lord would like to do with those experiences to help you become a better person, while allowing you to help someone else who may be going through a difficult time or similar situation.

Meditative Moments

There are times when your body is going to feel tight and tension occurs in your shoulders. Don't let this stop you from raising your arms and praising God.

Our meditative pose will be an arm stretch to open the shoulders and back.

This will help you stretch your shoulders and open your mind to the possibilities of letting go and feeling free. It will also help you in your daily routines of reaching for file folders carrying boxes, picking up your children and participating in your favorite athletic sport when using your arms, such as golf, bowling, praise-dancing, swimming, volleyball, baseball. This pose is helpful for relieving pain between the shoulder blades. It reminds us to keep that area open in the process of stretching the upper back.

Fold your arms placing your right hand on the upper part of your left and your left hand on the upper part of your right arm. Inhale and exhale. On the next inhale raise your arms while still folded to your forehead. Exhale arms down. Feel the stretch. Breathe and after a few breaths, raise the elbows up higher, over your head as to look between your arms. Remain grounded in the feet, whether you are sitting in a chair or standing. Relax the eyes, jaw, and tongue. Feel the expansion of the inhalation between the shoulder blades and the release on the exhalation. Lower the arms on the exhalation and repeat.

Benefits:
- Releasing tightness in the arms and shoulders.
- Assisting with opening the chest and back.
- Helps with breathing and balance.

Prayer focus: To be more thankful to God for others who sacrifice on my behalf.

Date: _____

Heavenly insight you have gained:

List a personal quality you are learning about yourself.

List two positive words of affirmation to speak into your life. Write what you anticipate to happen in your life from these words.

List the names of three people who you will encourage today. Purposely seek them out in order to enrich their lives with your influence.

The Law of Commitment

"Commit to the Lord whatever you do,
and your plans will succeed."
Proverbs 16:3

On Your Mark

It is a truth that most of us are not where we thought we would be at this time in our lives. In your own words what is a commitment? The foundation for, and the sustaining power of

The things you don't expect are often times the very things you should.

our commitment and achievement, comes when we surrender ourselves as we plan our goals in life.

Let's be honest, there we were at the starting block, getting into position, waiting for the official to give us our cue, and we got blind-sided by the little things that life dishes out to us. Or we put our hands in some things and royally messed it up! Other times, we failed to consider how a false start could stunt our growth. And then the reality of it all sets in. My life got twisted because I was in emotional turmoil or my last relationship left me in a broken and confused state of mind.

Help! I Have A Problem

Check all that apply:

☐ I am non-committal.
☐ I have people in my life who are non-committal.
☐ I know being non-committal is stunting my spiritual growth.

Take a moment and think how your responses are affecting your ability to live a balanced life.

Commitment is about embracing God's will and sticking with God through the ups and downs. And even though it seems that we are not able to make our way to the end with an anticipated outcome in mind, we stay the course because we have committed to doing so. The Law of Commitment is about balancing the expected with the unexpected.

In life you should expect to face adversity. We interact with people on a daily basis and that can often lead to seemingly unmanageable encounters.

And by dealing with others who themselves don't have it all together, we can be delayed by all the drama they are going through.

Other causes of unrest are circumstances that are out of our control. There are conflicts with family members, budget cuts on the job and unforeseen acts of violence, war, and terrorism. Your ability to ride the wave is monumental to your success. And greater still, being able to think on your feet and look at the situation from all angles will teach you to manage your stress levels.

While on a three-hour layover from Ridgecrest, North Carolina, to Milwaukee, I had an opportunity to hear about a testimony of a flight attendant whose husband was feeling the heat for attending a prayer meeting with some workers he supervised.

The factory workers attributed their success and no injury rate to the fact that they prayed daily as a team to perform well on the job. And as the wife told the story she intimated that when her husband would do inspections on a location that had a prayer group, he would sit in. The upper management of his company informed him that visiting those meetings was unacceptable of a mid-level manager. They told him that if he continued to visit the prayer meetings while doing site visits he would be terminated from his job.

I was amazed even further when she said that these meetings took place before the shift began and that the employees took it upon themselves to gather away from the plant to pray. The flights attendant's husband disobeyed the orders of his boss, and continued to attend the prayer meetings. He was eventually fired, leading him to file a legal suit against the company for violating his civil liberties. I applaud his conviction to be a man of integrity and not waiver in his faith.

How many of you have come under persecution for showing your commitment to Christ on your off time? Do you have what it takes to stand your ground, even if it means losing your job? Each of us will have to give an account, for Jesus said that he will not know you in the presence of his father, if you choose not to acknowledge him in the presence of mankind (Matthew 10:33).

Managing the Clock

The conflicts we face might not always be in the form of a tangled relationship. Yet, the conflict we ourselves may face, is a race against time. As you learn how not to waste time, you discover the importance of focus. The Proverbs writer admonishes us to *"let your eyes look straight ahead, fix your gaze directly before you. Make level paths for your feet and take only ways that are firm"* (4:25-26). When you are focused you are better able to manage your life and balance it against time.

Yes, you can begin to operate on a new dimension and in a new paradigm.

No matter how many ways you plan, you will continually find conflicts with scheduling. And if you are a perfectionist or a "timecruncher" you are in for many sleepless nights and restless days on the road to wherever you are trying to go. We are cautioned to *"not become weary in doing good, for at the proper time you will reap a harvest if we don't give up"* (Galatians 6:9). While walking to a business meeting with a lawyer friend, Melissa, we were discussing our husbands, travel, and the differences in our style of dealing with airports. We like to get to the airport early, our spouses not so much. She commented "Why would you build stress into your day when it will have enough of its own that you can't foresee!" I concur. Learning to keep time is important so you are not always running behind, have mental clarity about your options when time does go awry, and so you are making the most of every opportunity available. We must all exercise caution because time can run out on you.

Time management seminars tell you to build in moments of flexibility. Why? Because they know that nothing in life every goes according to plan, no matter how hard you try. It is always a sight to see people who pack their day so tightly that they are literally running from one place to the next, stressing themselves out because of this meeting and that family commitment. It is all a matter of accepting the reality of what impacts us and to build a cushion for the myriad of problems and unexpected little things that come up.

The things you don't expect are often times the very things you should. I know many of you will argue me down on the point of just not having to deal with some stuff, and it is that attitude that is going to keep you frustrated and steal your joy. You see life is about discovery, not destination.

We need to continually focus on committing ourselves to maintaining a natural flow through life and not always be under the gun. *"The prudent see danger and take refuge, but the simple keep going and suffer for it"* (Proverbs 27:12).

The Kick-er

Getting someone to change from being a tight scheduler to being able to build breathing room into his or her day is difficult. That's because too many people are resistant to change. You have to carry them off kicking and screaming to get them to understand that change is relevant to progress. The Psalmist tells us that our time is in God's hands (Psalm 31:15; Psalm 90:12). It will be wise for us to adhere to these words so that we are able to manage and focus appropriately when the occasion warrants.

Remember that uncommitted spirit? Our non-committal lifestyle, relationships and business practices can temporarily scar our ability to change for the better. Too often we want others to change so that we don't have too. But the question to be answered is, *"How long will you simple ones love your simple ways?"* (Proverbs 1:22). As you surrender to God, know for certain that He'll show you the way (Proverbs 4:11-13).

Our commitments are like fruitfulness. When we are fruitful our lives are productive and produce abundance to sustain us. But when we do not handle our time properly we are barren and our lives are empty and wasteful, and we are cast off as unable to be contributive. Matthew 7:18-19 records that *"a good tree cannot bear bad fruit, and a bad tree cannot bear good fruit. Every tree that does not bear good fruit is cut down and thrown into the fire."*

Hindrances to Commitment

In order to commit to change we must surrender ourselves by disregarding our old way of doing things and remove old habits and our old way of thinking.

Bishop Eddie L. Long of Atlanta's New Birth Missionary Baptist

Church once gave a sermon where he inferred that God has taken us to a new dimension in life, yet we are still living in an old paradigm. In essence, he was saying that the new dimension has positioned us to do some awesome things, yet we are still trying to do what we used to do to bring the new thing to reality. But that cannot happen because, as Matthew 9:16-17 states, *"we cannot add a new piece of cloth to an old one and neither can we add new wine into old wineskins."* No matter how we try new things with our old habits, we will be unproductive.

There is a new standard and precedent expected of you once you fully turn your life over to Christ. The Corinthian writer says *"so from now on we regard no one from a worldly point of view ... therefore if anyone is in Christ they are a new creation; the old has gone, the new has come!"* (2 Corinthians 5:16-17). And we can only get there by submitting ourselves as a living sacrifice.

I came to realize that I am not a stagnant person. I desire to live, move more freely and be a person of accomplishment on my journey. For it is in Christ that I live, move and have my being.

No matter how large or small, a win is a win with God!

On my quest, I remember that I have a responsibility to contribute as well as receive (James 1:22). Nothing in life is free. God expects me to do my part by cleaning up my act and being a respectable and responsible individual (Hebrews 10:24). I no longer have the luxury of surrendering to the ways of the world. Just because everybody else is doing it does not make it the right thing to do (Proverbs 14:12; Matthew 16:26; John 12:43; Romans 12:2; Colossians 3:2). We must all learn to exercise integrity in all we say and do. As I discover God's will and ways I am held more accountable than ever to God, others, and myself to no longer live according to society, my environment or culture.

Let's face it, when we live merely by comparing ourselves to others we devalue our own ability and God's will to achieve even greater things. Our comparison of ourselves to others is warped and overrated. And it is often the cause of our present struggle with past sin and misdeeds (Galatians 6:1-5; Hebrews 12:1-6).

Change Your Confidence

Living a more committed life first begins with believing you can. Yes, you can change your habits. Yes, you can reduce the stranglehold the Palm Pilot, Franklin Covey planner, Blackberry, Treo, and the Microsoft Outlook and Entourage calendar has on you. Yes, you can begin to operate on a new dimension and in a new paradigm! But it all begins with you changing confidence in yourself. Philippians 4:13 says, *"I can do all things through Christ who strengthens me."* That scripture is so true, but we have to believe with our minds and hearts that we can do all things.

We must learn to stop sticking to what we know and begin to challenge ourselves to explore new territory. Staying where you are gets you nowhere; listening to God's vision for your life, coupled with your boldness to step out on faith and believe can only make the vision of being a more confident person a reality.

Abraham is known as the father of the faithful because he learned the meaning of faithfulness and did not procrastinate. Abraham was not only a faithful man of God, but also a bold and courageous man because when God spoke to him about leaving his homeland (Genesis 12:1), he left knowing that he would be a stranger in a foreign land. Abraham could have easily said he wouldn't go. Yet he believed in God's word. He packed up his possessions and ventured off into unfamiliar territory with his wife, Sarai, and nephew, Lot.

If you look carefully at Abraham's story, he didn't seek out the advice of a friend or family member. Abraham was not Linked In, there was no Tweeting for others to follow his journey, no Facebook for him to get feedback from the crowd. He listened to God speak to him and boldly took action (Hebrews 11:8-10).

The law of commitment requires that we monitor and inventory the people who impact our decision-making ability. We have a tendency to rely heavily on the opinions of others rather than balance what is said to us against our own beliefs and value system. When we put too much emphasis on what others have to say, we can quickly fall into a state of despair, which negatively affects our families, community and ourselves (Galatians 6:1b).

We must be careful not to fixate on one, two or a group of people to shape our existence and then fall behind on personally developing our God-given way of living.

When Hezekiah was questioned by the king about his defiance towards him, he said, *"What is this confidence you have? Now on whom do you rely, that you have rebelled against me?"* (Isaiah 36:4; 2 Kings 18:19). Hezekiah knew he was following the will of God. He had the courage to defy the king because he answered to a greater King!

The Law of Commitment

When we embark on a new venture, whether it's a job, ministry or starting a family, our confidence and reliance should be on God to provide a clear and direct path for us to follow (Proverbs 19:20-21).

Too many opinions can cause our confidence toward our commitments to wane. Proverbs 21:16 says, *"a man who strays from the path of understanding comes to rest in the company of the dead."* How well can we recall friends with advice that came to a bad end!

Understand there are going to be times when our sources abandon us at critical junctures in our walk and we need to bear down on a sure thing: God. And when we feel deserted by our peers there is a tendency to abort our mission. Yet we know God is our dependable resource. Not only does He make avenues open for us, He provides us with a bonus by sending others to testify to us on our path to greatness. *"O Lord, I rejoice in your strength. How great is my joy in the victories you give!"* (Psalm 21:1).

I once had the daunting task of coordinating a fundraiser for a school of nearly 500 children. A venture of this size would require many hours and laborers.

As I called around and solicited volunteers from the community, met with parents and discussed the concept to the students, I realized that God had positioned the right people around me who could handle phone calls, do mail outs, and other tasks necessary to make it a success.

I didn't get caught up in the process. I did my part by following through with what God had given me, and he positioned the others to assist. And along the way, we all enjoyed the small victories.

If you are working on a large project and need to have people assist you, applaud yourself for finding all the people who can help, rather than focusing on the possibility of having to do it alone. If you are planning for an exam, don't think about the test, concentrate on the reading material. Or, if you are researching to write a Stimulus proposal, and seeking a community-based partner with whom to collaborate. When you have completed a few steps in the process – celebrate!

Whatever you are facing, God is in it with you and it is in our weakness that He becomes strong for and through us (Joshua 1:5). When we focus on the small victories and the way in which God orders our steps, we can rejoice over our accomplishments. No matter how large or small, a win is a win with God! (Proverbs 21:1).

Staying Out Of Harms Way

When I was younger, I used to hear the older people pray, "Thank you for keeping me while I slept in the very image of death; not for letting my bed become my cooling board and my covers my winding sheet." It took me a while to understand that not only do we sleep unknowing what's happening around us, but that in my blindness as a believer the devil is constantly setting traps for failure. As I travel in strange and unfamiliar places, I find myself praying that same prayer for the hotels I sleep in and the cab rides down unfamiliar streets.

Each day we walk into the fray as we go about our daily responsibilities. Every morning we wake to find that we are blessed beyond measure to be able to see another day, while at the same time placed in the presence of clear and present danger. The simple things in life are taken for granted as we complain about even smaller matters. It is here we find the dilemma of life. We get absorbed in the minutia of life and find that the devil has traps set to ensnare and trip us up. The enemy has one responsibility and this is *"to kill, steal and destroy"* (John 10:10a). Even though this may sound like three separate roles the primary emphasis is the same: break you down and erase you from the face of the earth.

In an effort to keep watch of the clear and present dangers around us Peter gives two ways to see the enemy before we get caught in his trap. *"Be self-controlled and alert. Your enemy the devil prowls around like a roaring lion looking for someone to devour"* (1 Peter 5:8).

We are to be self-controlled and alert. You can be sure every moment of everyday the enemy wants to hinder your progress. He takes your focus off work; he distracts you from prayer, or dishes out insults from your loved ones. Be aware. The devil is out there in many forms: in a nice suit, sexy dress, as a ball player, family member or friend, a job opportunity, business deal or sometimes just plain idleness.

Staying Focused

Most everything we do has its own motivation or stimulus that causes us to gravitate toward it. Atop the list of key motivators is love. Our relationships are built on it, fellowships are maintained by it and our service is driven by it.

Our conduct and behavior can be enhanced or hindered by

what we pursue in life. In our quest for a more committed lifestyle the four areas that must be continually surrendered to God are friends, family, faith, and our future. Any success we attain is for the maintenance of these four powerful and impacting areas.

As you consider your level of commitment to your life's journey, you will need to ascertain what you will in turn contribute. Our day-to-day interaction with others makes us watchful of how, when and with whom we associate. In an effort to stay committed and be aware of the enemy's schemes, a proactive stand is to be taken against the sly trickery.

We can gain ground when we:
- Run from compromising situations (1 Thessalonians 5:22).
- Stand strong; resisting temptation (Proverbs 1:10).
- Pursue godly values and attainable goals (Psalm 32:8).
- Search for significance in our life (Philippians 1:6).
- Keep our wounds in perspective (2 Corinthians 4:16-17).
- Expect to be tempted (I Corinthians 10:13).
- Have flexibility (Hebrews 6:11).

Galatians 6:1-10 gives us a glimpse of how we are to govern our lives in community with others. In our relationships we enjoy only one side of what they offer. We enjoy the fun, but can rarely stomach the heartache, hard work, and pain relationships bring.

I know people who are around for the birthdays, anniversaries, barbeques, and births and yet are absent at deaths, loss of jobs, sickness and other times of critical need. In your moment of rescue will you be a committed person whom others can depend on? Getting yourself together will allow you to be a blessing to others.

Journaling: The Law of Commitment

Once you have a healthier perception of God and release your misconceptions you will gain ground toward commitment to your goals and dreams. As you journal, think of people to pray for who need to become more committed. An added benefit to journaling is that you begin to grow in your prayer life.

Our prayer life, daily devotion and scripture reading ought to be off the charts. On the Heavenly Richter Scale we should register in at a 10 once we surrender ourselves fully to an empowered way of living. These steps offer practical helps to starting and maintaining a committed lifestyle. And as you grow along you should be moving toward a life filled with devotion to scripture, prayer and meditation. Here is how to have quality quiet time with God:

Devotion is a time of scripture reading, meditation, prayer and application. Select a passage or passages from the Word that are presently important to you. A good place to start is the Psalms, Galatians, Ephesians or Philippians. After reading selected verses ask yourself:

- How is this relevant to me?
- What is the intended learning of this verse in my life?

Listen to God's voice. Allow the Holy Spirit to reveal truth into your needs or give guidance for the day.

Pray on what is revealed. You may also find that many scripture lessons are preparing you for events that are yet to occur.

Apply what has been told or revealed to you. Watch God work throughout your day.

The key to your personal growth and ability is to stick with any empowerment change. Look at the methods and find those things that are relevant to where you are on various stages of your Christian journey, especially your intimate relationship with God.

Meditative Moments

A great posture for quiet reflection after reading or a tiresome day at the office is seated meditation, which allows for relaxation of the muscles and the mind.

Sit upright in chair with your rear-end to the back of the seat and your waist and shoulders properly positioned in the chair. Place your hands on your thighs close your eyes and simply inhale deeply through your nose. Hold your inhale to a five count and slowly exhale through your nose. As you repeat six times, allow your mind to relax and feel the weightlessness of your shoulders, back and neck.

Benefits:
- Allows for better posture
- Releases tension in shoulders, back and neck
- Clears the mind

Prayer focus: Learning to stay focused

Date: _____

〰〰〰〰〰〰〰〰〰〰〰〰〰〰〰〰〰〰〰〰〰〰〰〰〰〰

*A child is an adult in
training and it is our
responsibility to nurture.*

**Heavenly insight you have
gained:**

〰〰〰〰〰〰〰〰〰〰〰〰〰〰〰〰〰〰〰〰〰〰〰〰〰〰

List a personal quality you are learning about yourself.

**List two positive words of affirmation to speak into your life.
Write what you anticipate to happen in your life from these
words.**

**List the names of three people who you will encourage today.
Purposely seek them out in order to enrich their lives with your
influence.**

The Law of Harmony

"Whatever you have learned or received or heard from Me, or seen in me-put it into practice. And the God of Peace will be with you."
Philippians 4:9

I Decide

Harmony begins and ends with each of us. We know and understand that we must first be at peace with God and ourselves before we can go and face the world (Romans 3:8-10).

As a practice, when I wake each morning, I accept that my mind, physical body and spiritual senses are not completely working in unison. And in order for me to *"love the Lord with all my heart, soul and mind,"* I must work at keeping spiritually fit (Matthew 22:37). Each of my senses is independently working, but no community exists within my body that would allow me to just jump right up and encounter people with a glad and sincere heart.

I begin my day by continuing to lie down and allow my mind to become aware of my surroundings. The body has been in a rigid state for several hours and it needs time to adjust from a period of sleep. Remaining in bed awake not only allows my body to come alive, but also for my spirit to awaken to the possibilities of the new day.

As I lie down I get the blood flowing by pulling my knees one at a time to my chest and stretching my arms overhead, following it with a few deep breaths to cleanse my longs while pumping oxygen to my heart.

Silently pray and ask God to speak to your mind and heart so that He can show you His will for the day. You should also ask Him to show you or give you spiritual awareness.

Harmony is about understanding the process of mental, physical, and spiritual transformation. A spiritual transformation is where you recognize that *"our struggle is not with or against flesh and*

Life's' whatever moments should be our opportunity to spiritually realign ourselves.

blood, but against the wickedness, powers and principalities of this world" (Ephesians 6). Our transformation begins in our mind and leads us to put on the full armor of God to protect our body so that the Spirit can prevail and render us victorious and not incapacitated.

Harmony At Home

We spend a considerable amount of time outside of our home. And it is increasingly more and more difficult to strike a balance. We have a tendency to bring our frustrations from the outside inside our home. If this is your dilemma, then you truly have some issues that we need to pray about! Every person, married or single should have a place for personal quality time. Your home can become chaotic by allowing unwelcome spirits to flow within your dwelling place, or to take phone calls from people who can rapidly drive your blood pressure up.

Each of our homes should be a sanctuary away from all the hustle and bustle of life. And when we need it most, we have no place to turn to breathe, reflect, recover and begin anew.

In my home, my husband and I have made it clear that our bedroom will remain an oasis of love and affection. We don't have discussions about drama on his job, finances or anything else. We do not have a television, computer or stereo in our bedroom. We are committed to harmony in our bedroom. And it begins with no worldly distractions. We make a full effort for balance in every aspect of our life.

For those with children, your relationship with them can result in dissension.

Consider for a moment how you relate to them every morning – rushing them out of bed, letting them stay up too late, yelling at them and calling them names because they don't function at your level or on your time table. How cruel! A child is an adult in training and it is our responsibility to nurture. But if we as adults are unfocused and out of balance, then our issues are projected into their lifestyles, ultimately creating children with adult complexes.

The family is a unit that is supposed to be harmonious. That is not always the case, but we should work at keeping the peace. Constant nagging, playing, bugging and picking on each other can cause serious relationship problems. Bad family relationships can destroy its members. Our responsibility in the family is one of unity and connectedness because *"from Him the whole body, joined and held together by every supporting ligament, grows and builds itself up in love, as each part does its work"* (Ephesians 4:15-16).

Yet we cause ourselves to get bent out of shape over a variety of things, many of them relatively unimportant. And when that happens, we often get upset and that leads to an argument and an angry spirit (Proverbs 29;11; 29:22; 22:24; Proverbs 15:1-2).

Consider placing a check by the heart if these are an issue for you.

- Cap left off the toothpaste.
- Shoes left at that front or back door.
- Towels left on the counter.
- Walking on the carpet with outdoor shoes on.
- Not listening to the home voice mail.
- Chairs not slide all the way under the table.
- Gum wrapper left on the desk.
- Not answering the home phone on the second ring.
- Hanging the clothes in the closet in another direction
- Leaving the toilet seat up.

> ❧ Putting down the lid of the toilet.
> ❧ Placing the toilet paper under or over.

In the grand scheme of things, we should not set off World War III when one of these issues arises. We may allow them to annoy us and drive us batty, but we should always ask ourselves this question: Is it that important? We must learn the art being able to disagree without disrespecting.

Say It With Kindness

I am not suggesting that we give a friend, family member, child, or spouse a free license to do whatever they wish and we respond in a quiet and meek manner. No, we should be able to talk about issues that trouble us, but it doesn't always have to erupt into a full-scale fight.

When we speak, we should speak gently and calmly about the things that bother us (1 Corinthians 13:5; James 1:19). The Law of Harmony instills in us the value of kindness, compassion and community among those with whom we interact. What we say, how we say it and who we say it to can start incredible tension. The tongue is often referred to as a fire that can set a forest ablaze. No sooner than we have said something damaging, a great amount of destruction to another person can begin (James 3:1-18).

If we allow this to happen our Christian character and witness loses its credibility. With words we control our relationships with people; when used unwisely, words can hurt others by killing their Spirit, value and self-worth (Proverbs 10:19).

Our words can also make us hypocrites. How can we praise God with the same tongue we cuss out our children, spouses, bosses and friends or gossip about another's business? We take aim at others without considering the consequences. That then opens the door for areas in our own lives to come under attack. *"If someone is caught in any trespass, you who are spiritual, restore this person in a spirit of gentleness, each one looking to yourself, lest you to become tempted"* (Galatians 6:1-2; James 4). The goal is to not damage your own credibility and harm your chances toward a more meaningful and spiritually fulfilling life.

Me Now?

About right now some of you may be responding like a young girl I recently observed.

She and her mother were getting on the elevator when I heard mom say, "Your attitude is speaking so loudly, I cannot hear what you are saying."

The child replied under her breath, "Whatever!" I couldn't help but laugh at the scenario.

Do you possess a "whatever" spirit? "Whatever" used loosely carries highly negative connotations. When we are tired or fed up with a conversation we say, "Whatever." When we no longer desire another persons company, we say "whatever" when they asked us how we want to spend the evening. It even gets so bad that we physically and emotionally throw up our hands, smack our lips, raise our voice, and toss our head in disgust as we exclaim, "Whatever!" Cordiality has ceased to be the order in common, decent conversation.

But when it comes to our relationships with God, whatever shouldn't be a part of the communications process. We cannot and should not be so disgusted that we give up. Life's whatever moments should be our opportunity to spiritually realign ourselves. We should make an effort to reconnect with Him, others and ourselves.

Instead of blowing off the concerns with "whatever", we should apply Philippians 4:9 for understanding and reasoning.

- **Whatever is true.** Seek to know and then speak the truth about a matter before you step in.
- **Whatever is honorable.** Allow yourself to only participate in opportunities that will honor and glorify God.
- **Whatever is just.** Determine whether something should occur or not. Will it cause harm to another or dishonor your faith?
- **Whatever is pure.** Understand the motives and moral turpitude of your actions and others.
- **Whatever is lovely.** Seek to see the beauty of God in your words, behavior and that in others.
- **Whatever is commendable.** Never hesitate to do the right thing or give praise for doing well.

Harmony with others is such a valuable characteristic in our pursuit to fulfillment. If we cannot get along with those we love, how much more difficult is it to get along with people we barely know, such as our co-workers, church members and neighbors?

As you make it through this week, try these actions: The *first* is to think of one habit you have that is destroying your relationship with others and write it down. *Second*, find one person in your family or on the job that you will encourage. Do it whether you want to or not. Your lack of willingness to overcome a critical spirit will negate the harmonious atmosphere you are trying to create.

And *third*, learn to keep your mouth closed. Not everything that goes on around you requires you to speak on it. We have often heard that we need to pick our battles carefully. How true is it because God reminds us *"that the battle is not ours, but His"* (2 Chronicles 2:15).

If you find that you are unable to deal with life's stresses and controlling your tongue is difficult, you will find that improving your listening skills will help you focus your thoughts before you speak them. My sister-in-law Levita continually reminds her children 'they do not need to give voice to thought.' I know some adults who could put this wisdom phrase into action.

In every situation it is important to fully understand that clear communication is when people with issues meet people who can empathize with them or help them solve their problem. The problem begins when each person involved in the conversation has his or her own personal issues and no one is available who can bridge the gap between good and bad conversation (Proverbs 16:24; 18:15-17).

But another problem exists when there is a "know-it-all" in the group and others cannot get a word in. (Proverbs 18:2; 18:21). In order to balance yourself, consider these qualitative listening tips:

Let others see you are listening. Poised silence: do not interrupt when someone else is finishing a thought. Poised words: do not talk too fast, slow down as to select words carefully. (Proverbs 7:24)

Engage in constructive dialogue by asking questions. Find out what the person really wants and help the person vent their anger and frustration. Also help the person clarify their feelings. (Proverbs 8:33)

Review what you have heard so that the person knows you understand them. Put the message in your own words and include the main points for verification and clarity. Remain open to corrections. (Proverbs 1:21)

Out with the old, in with the new

So you have tried everything in your power to do the right thing and the stuff in your life is still messed up. Your life isn't about harmony but constant chaos. Well guess what? It might be time for you to make a drastic change to your situation.

Despite all that our mind and heart tells us, there are some people who we must cut loose in order to achieve harmony (Proverbs 12:26; 13:20; 16:28; 20:19).

Many of us have been in volatile relationships that tried our last nerve. We have been on our hands and knees, praying for that lost man or woman, yet they are still doing their own thing without any regard to us or God. We continue to pray to God to save the relationship, yet nothing changes. Then we assume that God doesn't care for us, when in fact he has answered our prayers. But we didn't like the answer!

Sometimes God is trying to get us to leave one situation because there is a better one around the corner that is devoid of the stress, drama and nonsense.

This also goes for your job. How many times in your life have you had a job that seemed to be sapping your energy, and the moment you left that job, all of a sudden it seemed like a burden was lifted off your shoulders? The Law of Harmony teaches us that we must rid ourselves of energy sapping and spiritually draining people or circumstances in order to live a more fully and complete life for God.

First Corinthians teaches us that we are not to be misled and that *'bad company corrupts good character"* (1 Corinthians 15:33).

Every time you try to do better, something or someone misleads you down the wrong path. You know you know better, but you keep running with bad company.

Often times we have the right mind to get it together and God intervenes every time we ask (Psalm 119:169-170; Psalm 141:1-2; 142:1-2; 6-7). He tells us what to do, how to do it and then gives us a way to escape from our burdens, but we sometimes fail to follow His lead because we are either entangled or co-dependent on or with someone else. As it turns out, the sooner we respect God's will and allow Him to guide us, grow us, and give us new life, the sooner peace is found (Psalm 119:103-104; Proverbs 3:13-18; 12:25; 14:30, 15:30; 16:24).

I trust today you will set yourself free from any bondage that is corrupting you. Make sure that the enemy is not leading you astray. Get on board with God and see brighter days.

Journaling: The Law of Harmony

Harmony is about our ability to apply the word of God to every aspect of life. It helps us work together with God to achieve the greater good. When you have a life that is about achieving peace, your life is filled with more rewarding experiences. However, a primary key to "harmonizing" is accepting scripture at its word and practicing its truths. As you write your thoughts, make every effort to be honest with yourself and what the Lord has revealed to give the joy and balance you deserve.

Meditative Moments

Achieving balance in your life is not going to be without its moments of tension. When you are tense and find you are being attacked on every side, consider our pose for the day to give you some relief. *A seated meditation using a chair* will offer you release from stress in your shoulders, back and neck. **Caution:** Move slowly if you have previous back, neck or shoulder injuries.

While seated, sit back in your chair as far as you can. Once in an upright position, extend your right arm across your chest to hold the left side of the chair. Gently turn your upper body to the right. Do not force a twist. Allow your body to turn naturally while keeping your feet planted firmly on the ground. If you need more flexibility sit with your feet and legs open to take any pressure off your hips. Hold your posture for a five second breathing count. Remember to inhale and exhale slowly through your nose. Transition by placing your left arm across your chest to hold right side of the chair and repeat the above instructions.

Benefits:
- Mental clarity
- Increases range of motion
- Relieves tension in hips
- Stretches the back
- Alleviates strain in shoulders and chest

Prayer focus: Those trying to break free to live a better life.

Date: _____

Heavenly insight you have gained:

List a personal quality you are learning about yourself.

List two positive words of affirmation to speak into your life. Write what you anticipate to happen in your life from these words.

List the names of three people who you will encourage today. Purposely seek them out in order to enrich their lives with your influence.

The Law of Readiness

"Therefore prepare your minds for action; be self-controlled; set your hope fully on the grace to be given to you when Jesus Christ is revealed."
1 Peter 1:13

Get In Gear

Our readiness begins with mental preparation. Unless we are mentally positioned for a blessing we will have difficulty operating within the structure of God's power; accepting direction and guidance from God and will be unable to maintain composure while on this life journey. Proverbs 1:32-33 says *"for the waywardness of the simple will kill them, and the complacency of fools will destroy them; but whoever listens to me will live in safety and be at ease, without fear of harm."* As you walk with God and he tells you what to do, you will want to be able to move about with confidence and fear no one. (2 Timothy 1:7)

With so many unknowns in life, how can one prepare and be ready for what will come next? Is there any value to having awareness before hand so that when opposition comes, it can be faced with confidence and a cool head? Absolutely yes!

The true keys to readiness are obedience, discipline and appropriate behavior. The spiritual implications for each allow you to honor God with an attitude of gratitude. It also helps you focus your priorities and ready yourself for what is coming your way.

Obedience. Hearing and following instructions from God is expected of believers. In order to be completely ready for the journey, you must *"obey God's teachings."* (John 14:23)

Discipline. To have discipline is to be consistent in the practices one is taught. It is the same as a disciple: a follower and learner of Christ who also embraces the concepts of what is taught and applies them to daily living. It is when we *"hold to the teaching...we will know the truth that sets us free."* (John 8:31)

Appropriate behavior. We are able to conduct ourselves in the world without bowing down to the ways of the world. Appropriate behavior implies that we are able to show mercy when mercy is needed, correction when appropriate, kindness when warranted, and faith at all times in every situation. Paul says *"our conscience testifies that we have conducted ourselves in the world...in the holiness and sincerity that are from God"* (2 Corinthians 1:12).

If you have ever been blind-sided or caught completely off guard, then you understand why a lack of preparedness, when coupled with unawareness, could be considered a primary downfall in personal achievement, loving relationships., and business ventures.

The parable of the man who built his house upon the sand gives testimony of the foolishness of people who go off half-cocked. Hearing and applying the instruction of God and wise counsel prevails every time. Consider this: *"Everyone who hears these words of mine (God) and does not put them into practice is like the foolish man who built his house on the sand. The rain came down, the streams rose, and the winds blew and beat against that house, and it fell with a great crash"* (Matthew 7:27-28).

Is your life falling with a great crash? In order to lay a firm foundation and get on the right road towards positioning and purpose, we must first ready ourselves for the work involved. God has promised and committed to ready us. His word says, *"I guide you in the way of wisdom and lead you along straight paths. When you walk, your steps will not be hampered; when you run you will not stumble. Hold on to instruction, do not let it go; guard it well, for it is your life"* (Proverbs 4:11-13).

Yes, life is work. To make lasting strides in life it requires:

- **Diligence.** To be consistent and determined to continue in a practice (Hebrew 6:11).

- **Patience.** It is a virtue, a fruit of the spirit and means to endure under trial (Galatians 5).

- **Vision.** To see as God sees and to be given insight toward specific duties and tasks; to have focus (Proverbs 29:18).

The same tenacity that we bring to a project on the job should also be brought to reaching deep within to better our lives.

In order to seek that complete fulfillment you should have a clear understanding of your relationship with God and His will for your life.

It would be easy to talk about future plans, being ready to take it to the next level and all that, but if your foundation is uncertain then your efforts will be fruitless. As recorded in Psalms 127:1, *"Unless the Lord builds the house, its builders labor in vain."* And as anyone who has built a home fully comprehends that building on a solid foundation is critical to the home being able to withstand and endure the elements!

The experiences we have in life – the good, bad and indifferent – shape our outlook and outcome (Proverbs 24:3). We often say that some issues caught us by surprise, but if the truth be told, we saw it coming days, weeks, months, even years ahead of time. Yet we refused to get out of the way or do anything about it (Proverbs 16:18). Many of the stresses we have and our inability to cope comes from guilt, shame and disobedience in matters we should have handled a long time ago (Proverbs 13:18).

A Balancing Act

Peace of mind in the midst of adversity is critical to preventing various health problems, including high blood pressure, stroke, heart attack, panic attacks, shortness-of-breath, blackouts and hyperventilation. We must settle ourselves in order to achieve our goals. We are cautioned that *"even in laughter the heart may ache, and joy may end in grief"* (Proverbs 14:13). We must be careful to not continually over exert or extend ourselves.

A series of self-discovery exercises can help you focus and become more balanced within. Through stress relief techniques such as prayer-walking, stretching, visualization and breathing you can reach God's desired state of peace and tranquility for your life. However, unless you work on the root cause of your issue you will never be completely free from future attack or complexities. You must get under control those areas in your life which cause you envy and strife (Proverbs 16:17; Proverbs 22:17-21).

An old cliché says the mind can play tricks on us. We hear what is not spoken. We see what is not there. We miss what never was nor intended to be.

A big portion of our existence is spent pining away after things that were never meant to be ours. I understand that a perceived reality can be better than the reality we are actually living. For some, what is real can be too harsh to deal with.

Another primary source of our inability to cope and manage stress is due in part to our inability to master our emotions. Doing so involves monitoring the people who we allow to influence our lives. As our emotions get out of hand they ultimately get out of control. And a life out of control does not possess the ability to pump the brakes on life's roller coaster at the appropriate time.

I recall while in seminary how sick I became one day while sitting at my desk. I couldn't breathe, and had chills and was unable to talk or walk. Upon passing out students from class rushed me to the emergency room.

> *Life is too short for intentional unpleasantness.*

As the nurse prepped me for a test she stuck me in my arm with a needle. It flew out of my arm splattering blood across my gown and the hospital walls. My blood pressure was so high that my body was virtually a balloon ready to pop. And, it did!

Stress had an unmerciful grip on me and I didn't even know it.

I was a full-time seminary student, holding a full-time ministry staff position and traveling as a speaker. I thought my late 20s body could handle all that I was throwing at it, but it let me know who was the boss. The time had come when enough was enough and I had to take control before I destroyed my body and ultimately my life. I know what can happen to a life that runs ahead of God one time too many. In this resource you have been asked to come face-to-face with your personal concerns.

In order to live a balanced and fulfilling life you must seek to balance your loads of life. Of course *"the Lord will not put on us more than we can bear"* (1 Corinthians 10:13), and we must pay close attention to when we are close to being overwhelmed. In an all out effort to keep it together, here are a few helpful holy hints for your consideration.

Redefining Your Life on Your Own Terms

1. Discover what makes you tick.

2. Know the truth about yourself and never give up.

3. Stay away from people who tear you down.

4. Guard yourself from predators.

5. Seek the best. Never settle.

Your loads in life will have varying weights, but God has made them (Proverbs 16:11). Life is stressful and there is no way getting around the fact that we have to live it, regardless of how compounded it gets. So what are you going to do? Give up? Give in? Cave into our fears of past unsuccessful outcomes? I think not! Understanding and evaluating past events in your life will act as a catalyst to managing and planning for a healthier and more productive future.

Your ability to humble yourself will cause your greatness to rise within you. Scripture records, *"My heart is not proud, O Lord, my eyes are not haughty; I do not concern myself with great matters or things too wonderful for me. But I have stilled and quieted my soul; like a weaned child with its' mother, like a weaned child is my soul within me"* (Psalm 131:1-3).

As you grow with the Lord you discover the virtues of living a humble life. You are able to be more aware and sensitive to your surroundings and how you are impacted by the activities around you.

Our five senses play a key role in our trek to wellness and it is the nurturing of our spiritual senses that guide the physical senses to a more harmonious interlude; a state of readiness beyond measure.

How To Achieve Positive Outcomes

There is no doubt that the enemy is going to make attempts at foiling your plans to a more balanced life, but don't give up without a fight. I too have ambitions and expectations. Yet I know that I cannot do it all by myself. For me, letting go and letting God handle all my affairs sends the message that I truly trust God and am willing to follow His lead.

My husband has a simple statement that he applies to all of his endeavors: "Let God and get out of the way!" Timing plays a major part in our readiness levels as well. In Genesis, Chapters 39-41, the story of Joseph depicts the most vivid picture of how timing impacts our lives.

Timing is defined as the precise moment at which something happens for maximum impact or effect. In our lives it translates into how our will and Gods' will connect to perform the purposes for which we were created. This is why timing is important. Time deals with six critical areas of readiness:

- God's availability to protect us when we are doing what we are supposed to be doing
- God's ability to provide for us what we need in time of need
- God's way of teaching us lessons before we go off doing things we are not yet ready for
- God's persistence in leading us where we have to go for our greater good and His glory
- God placing restrictions on us so we don't get too far ahead of Him and ourselves
- God graduating us when we least expect it

Timing with God is perfect, and when we understand how it works we are able to control ourselves and prepare for what is ours to achieve.

But again, we must get out of our comfort zones in order to achieve positive outcomes in every aspect of our lives, whether it's with family members, marriage, the job or even at church.

Yet far too many of us are accustomed to either not rocking the boat or saying anything out of turn. All that does is silence our own voice and stifle our opinion making.

We live in a time when we cannot afford to stand idly by. If we are silent, when we are supposed to speak up, we miss out on opportunities to set the record straight for others and ourselves.

As you come to accept and appreciate the eight spiritual laws of fulfillment, know that each law is designed to tug at the heart of your circumstance, or as said in Philemon 7, *"Your love has given me great joy and encouragement, because you, my brothers and sisters, have refreshed the hearts of the saints."*

I have worked diligently to find my own sense of peace and solace in the midst of the world's adversity. As a frequent flyer and avid traveler, whether I am in the car, on a plane or sailing the beautiful seas, I find my thoughts being invaded by the brevity of a moment. I am learning to enjoy, even more than usual, the cool breeze of a winter afternoon, the bright sun warming my face on a cloudless day, or adoring my husband as he gently and quietly sleeps.

Life is precious so I value the simple things in it, such as the walks in the park, the stages of the moon on a clear night, the stars twinkling in the sky or the first time a toddler expresses a new character trait.

The tendency to take others for granted, to misuse the kindness

of a co-worker or abuse the trust of a friend is no longer accept-
able behavior. Life is too short for intentional unpleasantness.

Mentally, physically, spiritually and emotionally, we must discover ways to free our mind from the uncertainties in life and focus on the God who knows all things, is everywhere and has all
the power to make things well.

Great Adaptations

As we adapt, we come to respect the new things God offers to us.
I believe that in whatever situation you find yourself, you should
know how to make the necessary adjustments work. Life is about
adjustments. And the Law of Readiness demands that we make
every effort to be prepared for what may come our way.

Making the proper adjustments means:

Evaluating your situation. You need to know how you will
function in your new role and what inhibitions you have.

You will need to talk it over with people close to you. It will
do you good to be on one accord with the people that live in your
house. There will be a new way of doing things and equally more
responsibility will be given to you.

Give yourself time. You will need time to settle in to your new
way of life. Communicate how you feel with your loved ones. It is
possible that your family will try to take you for granted, and you
must be firm about everyone's expectations.

Paul has made it clear that through all things, we will have to prevail. Your ability to make the best of your situations will provide you with the tools to use as stepping-stones to advance your growth and spiritual maturity. With each passing day, for every hurdle you overcome, you will be able to face each new challenge with confidence, certainty, and competence.

Journaling: The Law of Readiness

As you express your thoughts today, consider your personal level of readiness for life's journey.

You may need to re-think your plans or simply follow a checks and balances procedure to make sure you are on track. Whatever you need, I am certain that you will find the peace and strength you need for a joyous journey.

Meditative Moments

Once you have your mind ready, your body may be saying, "no." You may find yourself physically exhausted and immobile from lack of activity. In order to keep your mind and body on one accord, our meditative posture for the day will be for *balance*.

You can begin by standing with your back placed firmly against the wall, arms loosely by your side. Allow yourself to feel your body composition. You will want to know if your shoulders lean to one side or another, if your knees tighten when you stand, if your hips or lower back sway and if you stand with your head tilted to one side or another. Once you are stable inhale and exhale to a five second count, breathe three times.

You may notice that when you are standing in a line you have to rest on the counter, cross your ankles or stand with your legs apart to keep from teetering over. As you practice this posture you will find you have greater balance and will not have to make such adjustments. You will also find that you are doing more with your life because it is no longer a problem for you to stand.

Benefits:

- Better posture
- Alleviate strain in lower back
- Helps in breathing
- Aids in digestion

Prayer focus: Those who need to get on with living.

Date _____

Heavenly insight you have gained:

List a personal quality you are learning about yourself.

List two positive words of affirmation to speak into your life. Write what you anticipate to happen in your life from these words.

List the names of three people who you will encourage today. Purposely seek them out in order to enrich their lives with your influence.

The Law of Creativity

"For I know the plans I have for you, declares the
Lord, plans to prosper you and not to harm you,
plans to give you hope and a future."
Jeremiah 29:11

God is Waiting on You

We often think that *"train up a child in the way they should go and when they are old they will not depart from it"* (Proverbs 22:6) only applies to being reared in Christian instruction. But it also speaks to following the path to our destiny that the Lord has designed and created us to achieve.

God will use a vessel that is willing to be used. I have discovered that God is less concerned with my ability, but more so with my availability.

As we avail ourselves to Him, we are able to sit at the feet of Jesus and learn what is needed for our journey ahead. I learned early on that my salvation called me into service and upon that calling I was given certain spiritual gifts to fulfill that responsibility (Ephesians 4:11-12). No matter where in life you meet God, I now know that even as damaged goods, sometimes damaged goods are more valuable because of their unique qualities that God can and will use.

Where are your passions? What do you desire to do with your life? I have watched Sister Act II over and over again to see the disdain in the character Ms. Ralph played as mother of Lauren Hill. A truly gifted and talented young person willing to work and put in the effort and time to achieve her dreams, would have them constantly deferred by a parent who could not see past her own personal problems. The same in The Secret Life of Bees that the hurt and pain of a troubled past kept both June and May from being free to live freely.

Have you not been able to do what you wanted? Or become what you believed you were intended to be? If so, you are not alone. Millions of young people each day are being pressed and molded into what others want them to become. But that is not the way of God. Our ability to be creative comes from following the natural and spiritually given bent that God has placed within us. Our creativity is in our willingness to follow God and use the gifts we have been given. Consider the character 'Precious' in the movie.

It is with the giving of spiritual gifts to each one who claims Jesus as Lord that our strategy and purpose for living is made plain. Gifts are given by God, Jesus and the Holy Spirit, as noted in 1 Corinthians 12:4, Romans 12:3, and Ephesians 4:7. When we are open to God leading our lives, our destiny enables us to balance everything else around the primary thing we are to be doing in life. Yet there are times when we are led astray and getting back on track is difficult.

There comes a point in everyone's life when the road on which we travel seems to be paved with tears over broken dreams, shattered hopes, jilted relationships, financial hurdles, societal ills, family crisis, personal indiscretions, professional favoritism and a slew of other traumas and 'isms'.

These varying sets of circumstances, when combined with a degree of vulnerability, can alter your course in life. For some, that means a point of no return, which can leave you devastated. If you are at that place where you feel like there is no hope and you are just treading water, start proclaiming the mantra of Fannie Lou Hamer who, after suffering the indignities of a segregated society, said in the 1960s that she was "sick and tired of being sick and tired."

So many of us reach the point of no return when we feel as if we have nothing to lose and we just say, "No more." That's when we stand up to the drama and ready ourselves to get out of the mess in which we find ourselves.

It was not until I embraced and absorbed my past that I realized the amount of baggage I was carrying around with me. It is when we reach a true breach of all trust that we are ready to do things Gods' way.

Here are seven truths about my life that God revealed to me as a path to follow for my creativity to begin to flow:

1. Acknowledge you have a need that cannot be filled by material means.
2. Bring yourself to the altar and surrender your emptiness.
3. Confess and believe in your heart that God sent His only Son for you.
4. Deny yourself daily and take responsibility for your actions and follow Christ.
5. Examine your life and surrender your ways and means to Christ.
6. Forever trust and never doubt God.
7. Accept God is faithful and will honor His word.

I have continued to find peace in the Master's arms as He refines my life and brings me forth as a new creation. Each of our situations, once we get to the root cause is remarkably similar. We have misplaced ambitions that are self-led rather than God-led which lead to unbalanced lives and lifestyles. And once we are aware that our seeking is displaced, we can turn our efforts toward becoming the kind of vessel God can use.

A Vessel God Will Use

While God is waiting on us to allow Him complete and unfettered access to our lives, we must get out of the way and let him lead.

Jeremiah records that God has plans for us and that he will not harm us while pursuing and achieving that end (Jeremiah 29:11). The problem is that we think and have often sought to assist God with those plans, thereby making our will, the will of God.

Our passion and pursuit of relentless control over every area of our lives cannot only be damaging to us, but those around us. Oswald Chambers once said, "Those whom God uses greatly, must first be broken deeply."

It is out of our brokenness that we find our true path in life. After all the mistakes, heartache and pain we finally can see the road that was meant for us to travel. It is on this road that we understand we are called to a purpose in life that we have been divinely designed to pursue.

God endows each of us with gifts and extraordinary talents to use not only for his glory, but also for providing us with balance and substance in an otherwise empty existence.

You will have reached a new level in your faith journey once you have completely surrendered. Your faith acts as the catalyst to propel you toward the plans God has for you. In case you have not noticed, you are uniquely and "wonderfully made" (Psalm 139). Congratulate yourself for being a chosen vessel of God and remember you are able to see to completion what God has prepared for you to do.

You will never be the person God has called you to be until you trust and obey the way He chooses to supply your life with spiritual and material wealth. The sooner you respect the will of

God and allow Him to guide your growth, the sooner you will find peace and fulfillment.

Years ago, I lost a fiancé to leukemia three months before we were to be married. I was devastated and did not know how to keep it together. I had already resigned from my pastoral staff position and was preparing to move out of state to serve alongside him as first lady and co-pastor of his church in Alabama. A little girl's dream of marriage and family was on the horizon, yet that was shattered.

When he died I had to undue my plans and emotionally figure out how to move on. God began to use this encounter as an open door to heal and help others. He is *"the Father of all compassion and the God of all comfort, who comforts us in all our troubles, so that we can comfort those in any trouble with the comfort we ourselves have received from God"* (2 Corinthians 1:3-4).

I started doing grief counseling and preaching to young men and women who lost fiancés, some very tragically. From this traumatic experience a grief ministry was birthed as I began working with funeral homes, starting support groups and speaking to various corporations on helping employees deal with various levels of loss so that they can function day-to-day.

His death did not deter me, it re-focused me.

I have learned that fulfillment begins where our will ends. God has since positioned me as a Christian life skills coach. It has always been my passion to assist people with applying God's word to every day occurrences. Had I been obstinate, pressed the matter of having my way and doing what I thought was best, rather than letting God guide me, I would not be enjoying the life I now live (Proverbs 23:12).

I believe I am suppose to champion all of the adversities in my life. In doing so, I have discovered the ability of allowing Christ's teaching to govern my life and letting the Holy Spirit guide me toward God's intended purposes.

I soon began to accept that I was a vessel that God was willing to use and that my pain and suffering would not be in vain. God was challenging me to turn my misery into a ministry. In other words, my trial became my testimony.

This trying moment reminded me of so many people in scripture God used to pull off some of the most extraordinary feats in the world (Hebrews 11).

As I read the book of Hebrews, I realized the people in the chapter of faith were ordinary people who excelled under the auspices of extraordinary stress. And whether we believe the accounts or not, it does not change the miraculous nature of the outcomes. God says, *"See, I am doing a new thing!"* (Isaiah 43:19). The sovereignty of God is beyond our scope and control. So why are we so amazed when God calls our name? He can do what he wants, when he wants, and with whomever wants. After all, *"We are His, the sheep of his pasture"* (Psalm 95:6-7).

Our ability to become balanced is based on how we perceive the work the Lord has planned for us, while at the same time fully understanding that it is His work. Not all of our work is easy, but all work for the Lord is rewarding, *"for it is the Lord who works in us both to will and to do His good pleasure"* (Philippians 2:13).

There are certain characteristics indicative of the personality traits of a person who is moving forward toward living a fulfilled life:

Ambitious. There is nothing wrong with seeking the greater good for your life. Our ambitions should cause us to lead a life that enhances and enriches others, rather than hinder or destroy everything in our path. The disciples followed Christ at any cost and the women in scripture were able to partner in sharing the

Gospel by providing financial resources, teaching, preaching, and working alongside others' in the faith.

Cooperative. Our attitude about the work set before us must be conducive to getting the job done. When we complain about our assignments we can act as a hindrance to pure productivity. Many hands make light work, this way everyone benefits from the labor.

Responsive. When it is time to do your part, will you come running with enthusiasm or hide behind your fears? We each have a duty to do our fair share in the family, community, workplace and church. God is calling us to be on call for his glory!

Here's Hope

Being a Christian is a life-long process. It means totally surrendering every aspect of your life to God's care, custody and control. It involves accepting Christ, following His led, following His people and continuing to surrender your will to His will.

As your creativity flows, your vulnerability shows and you soon get to a point where nothing is sacred about your life or embarrassing. I have long sense ceased to be embarrassed about the happenings in my life. I understand that where my past ends, my transparency begins. People, like me, who are searching for solace in their harried lives, often ask how can someone know the will of God and if the pursuit of fulfillment is a part of God's plan. Knowing His will means hearing with your heart rather than your ears (Proverbs 3:5-6). God speaks to us all day long through our daily activities. In every area of engagement you will find God has been and is a part of it.

We fail to recognize that God is gentle and will not overwhelm us every time He needs our attention. Not all of us need to have a Damascus Road experience like the Apostle Paul, where we have to be knocked out cold before God has our undivided attention. Sometimes it is like Elijah that God speaks in the whisper or the cry of a small child or the elderly couple strolling through the park holding hands. God chooses to use the method that will impact us the most at the time we need to hear what He has to say. Roland often tells the story of how we met, smiling as he states "God had her wear the right pair of black pants on the right day. Those long preacher robes were not getting me to pay attention the way God needed me to pay attention."

Often times when God speaks it is to give us guidance, direction, confirmation, affirmation and warnings. Think back to your last action. How did it come about? How were you prompted to pursue it? What were your feelings? Did you get a feeling of peace and calm as you went forth? This is God speaking and reaffirming His will. However, if you meet obstacles along the way or were nervous and uneasy this may be a trap. As we grow in our faith and discover how to respond to God faithfully, we see our obedience being brought under attack. The enemy will try to trick you in order to move you away from God. And as the devil works his plan, you will find yourself further and further away from God's design and intended purpose for your life.

As you journey with the Lord you become increasingly aware of what is and is not of God.

A Person of Fulfillment

Our quest for fulfillment is steeped in God's love for us. By creating us in His image we are instruments of His glory chosen for a great work that He will ensure comes into fruition. The present situation you face that seems dismal and full of despair is the opportunity being used at this moment to turn your life around. Will you face your crossroad so that an inroad can be made toward your personal fulfillment? Sure you are enjoying yourself, yet are unable to sleep at night. You can't be alone with yourself without feeling lonely. Be at peace in the company of people who are different than you. God will teach you how when you let him fully in your life.

This is my personal covenant with God in order to be a person of fulfillment.

Each of us is given a moment in time to accept God's call

- I will be a person of substance
- I will allow God access to my heart.
- I will put a new principle into practice daily.
- I will enhance another life along the way.

Understanding yourself allows you to see the positive difference you can make in the world, starting immediately with those around you. While developing my personal statement of affirmation, I found my creativity being fueled by my positive outlook. I can now hold myself accountable by operating within my personal belief system about my life and God's will.

A personal statement of affirmation begins with understanding your roles in life. You could be a mother, father, uncle, aunt, student, wife, daughter, a church leader or a vast array of other resources. The key is to know those key roles and design ways according to God's word on how to live out those roles while facilitating growth in others.

Journaling: The Law of Creativity

As you prepare to journal, pray to find people whose lives could be turned around simply because you encourage them to find balance in their lives.

Meditative Moments

Have you ever had days when your creative juices were no longer flowing? There are times when you need to stretch your mind, while alleviating tension to be restored. Our posture will be a standing forward bend, while using a chair as a prop.

Get a chair and place it with the back of the chair facing you. Stand upright. Gain your balance. Make sure your legs are spread shoulder distance apart to eliminate the possibility of injury to your back. Once balanced lean forward, bend gently from the hip resting your arms on the back of the chair. As you bend forward, cross your arms placing each hand on your elbows. Rest your head on your arms relaxing your mind and clearing your spirit through deep breathing.

Benefits:

- Stretches the hamstrings and releases the back
- Calms and cools the spirit
- Allows your mind to rest without visual distractions

Prayer focus: Those needing reassurance.

Date _____

Heavenly insight you have gained:

List a personal quality you are learning about yourself.

List two positive words of affirmation to speak into your life. Write what you anticipate to happen in your life from these words.

List the names of three people who you will encourage today. Purposely seek them out in order to enrich their lives with your influence.

The Law of Empowerment

*"The Angel answered, "The Holy Spirit will come
upon you, and the power of the Most High will
overshadow you, so that the one to be born will be called
the Son of God."*
Luke 1:35

Positioned for Presence

God has long since desired to do something great through you. But because you were out of position your abilities could not be used. Consider your need for a breakthrough that could only come by you having to endure an arduous situation. Seemingly at the onset you did not like the set up, but as time went on you began to appreciate more and more what God had in mind.

There are many great people among us who were not always so great. They started out as ordinary people doing ordinary things, but they decided to work on God's extraordinary plan.

Each of us is given a moment in time to accept God's call to do the right thing at the right time no matter the odds. Consider Peter and his command in the book of Acts. The people were stunned that Peter, an ordinary man, was infused with God's power and anointed for the work he was accomplishing. Biblical history continues to pave the way as our example. The book of Esther gives an empowering and liberating testimony of how our personal joy of being in a certain position can lift us to a greater purpose and role in life.

When we least expect it all of the pieces of our life seem to fall in place.

It is here that the Law of Empowerment is about what God wants accomplished and not about what we ourselves can gain.

The account of Esther and her role in the life and times of her people leads us to an understanding of how we are empowered when we have the tools and resources needed to prevail in any situation. God's placing Esther as Queen would soon find thousands equally empowered and liberated.

I enjoy that a new queen needed to be chosen because Queen Vashti refused to be exploited for the pleasure of men and at the request of her husband. There are times that we have to defy tradition in order to preserve the honor of God and ourselves. Esther was able to become queen because of the honor and integrity of her predecessor.

As you read the Book of Esther five truths leap from the pages of biblical history for our guidance and growth for today:

- **Picked by her people (2:8).** Esther was an orphaned woman of mediocre means. She could have easily found herself in a pity party thinking she would not be able to enter the running for queen. How often do we look at our past or present circumstance and make a judgment about our future? Esther was fortunate to have a supporting guardian who encouraged her to stay in the game of life. It is noted that she was a beautiful woman, *"lovely in form and features."* To the contrary most pretty women are not self-absorbed. Many of them suffer from poor self-esteem and an inaccurate portrait of their true worth. Esther was to embark on the adventure of a lifetime, despite her personal perception of herself.

- **Prepared by God** (2:9). How many times have you been told look before you leap? We must take care to go into life altering affairs with conservation and awareness. As Esther was escorted to a life of newness, she would soon find favor with those in charge of her care. She was treated with respect and honor from the moment she entered the palace. Was it because of her inward or outward features? Or could it have been that God was preparing the way for her to do something extraordinary? Charming when not on guard, Esther excelled in her new environment and quickly began to use her favor to her advantage. She was not manipulative, abusive or evasive. She simply took the advice of her advisors.

- **Positioned in troubled times (4:11-14).** No one but God knew what was in store for Esther. What is important to know is that regardless of why she was being taught certain things, Esther learned to follow instructions, master the way of the palace and soon found herself ready to go before the king. Each time I read Esther I am reminded how we can glean a process from her life to move more effectively in our lives. In order to be positioned for our intended purpose we must go through a few grueling stages. Consider the discipline associated with getting to the level we believe we should be operating on. The accounts of Esther indicate a 12-month regiment. We often have difficulty going through 12 hours of training let alone a year. Are you willing to go the distance in disciplining yourself for greatness?

- **Propelled for greatness** (4:15-17). As Esther took her position as queen she soon was confronted with a task that conflicted with her personal outlook as queen. Isn't that just like life? As soon as we arrive at our desired station in life, we are exposed to a situation that could send us careening from the top of the ladder. Esther had it all – beauty and brains – and she was challenged to show her brawn. Esther was about to reveal something about herself that she had never told anyone. Was it in her? Was she up for the challenge? Would she consider not stepping up to her responsibility? Yes on all counts. It didn't take Esther long to realize the greater work she had been sent to accomplish.

Esther is a person whom God could use. She was open to the situation around her and was not overly skittish about getting her hands dirty. On the contrary she even consented to die for the cause. Your empowerment comes when you are willing to let go of self and embrace the plans God has for you.

One summer while in conference, the minister espoused a litany that will keep you thinking as it did the audience who listened on. What happened to the church that fell in love with God? Where are the people who claim to be His followers? The questions stuck in my head as a lump formed in my throat. Even the church that does great things for each other and great things for God does not have it all together when it comes to living up to their full potential. "We seem to have the attitude of the world" he continued, "no one fears God anymore." How right he was as the Lord revealed to me that it is time that we stop settling for the simple wages of the world and prosper as the Lord has promised we would as workers in His field.

Are you using your gifts and talents in an honest manner? Have you gotten rich and have the rewards of the world because you swindled someone? We must be careful not to become empowered for ill-gotten gain, but to build up the weak and lowly with our resources, skill and passion.

God Made You Special

How you feel about yourself determines how far you will go in life. If you feel as if no one takes you seriously you will become shy and reserved. If you believe you are constantly overlooked you will fail to take risk to achieve greater things. If you are told that your opinion does not matter you will discontinue striving to make a difference. If you feel as if you have nothing to contribute you will cease to make an effort to show up at all. Each of these statements can cause us to feel useless and helpless. It becomes important when seeking balance and joy for a fulfilled life that we understand that our greatness does not come from other people, but from God.

In our quest to rise above the meaningless things in life we are to do so because we trust and believe that we are special and created for a purpose. No longer are we discouraged by unkind words or the lack of opportunities presented to us. We are well on our way to creating avenues of success, not only for ourselves but also to the generations that will follow. Consider the momentum of the 2008 election as thousands stood breathless in Grant Park when the final polls closed and ballots were being counted. Recall the electrifying day on Capitol Hill as the world stood still for the Inauguration of President Barack Obama. We are leaving a legacy behind, but in order to get to the legacy-leaving-stage, we must first come to terms with what is expected of us. As we seek fulfillment and as God is calling us to greatness, we must understand the process of what He will take us through to get us to where we are destined to be and become.

Going the Distance

In our walk with God we see the mystery and miracles of our faith in Him. Something happens when God calls our name. We often experience uncertainty about the path to take or not fully comprehend the plan that is laid out for us.

Consider the encounter of Mary and the angel Gabriel in Luke Chapter 1. The Law of Empowerment is birthed from this story. Not only do we have the coming of Christ as promised, but we are able to see the dialogue that took place to get Mary to the point of her empowerment to endure her coming trials. For what started out as a trial is a triumph for us all!

When we least expect it all of the pieces of our life seem to fall in place. But notice how all of it is orchestrated. It seems to Mary that the angel just appeared out of nowhere, but that is not so.

Prayer must be the central focus of my endeavors.

Earlier verses record that God gave the angel specific instructions on where to find Mary. The angel was sent to a certain town, in a specific region to look for a particular girl by a designated name. I love it! God knows our address. When God is ready to bless you, He knows exactly how and where to find you. And not only will He find you, He will answer all your questions about what He intends to do with you.

But Mary wasn't being all holy and pious. She had a ton of questions for the angel. In verse 29 an amazing dialogue begins. Mary is caught off guard by the fact that this stranger knows her name. More so than by what the angel tells her, she wants to know how she can be in favor with God.

Mary was a young girl with little experience in life. She was barely out of her parents' home and had not found a job or time to become acquainted with the society in which she lived.

How true it is for us when we are branching out on our own. We have some idea of what to do, but are rarely ready for a major assignment right out of the shoot. But God knows our intended purpose in life and will seek to help us find the tools we need for the journey. Mary was afraid and needed reassurance that she could do what was being presented to her.

After a few rounds of conversation and a very detailed explanation of the vision God planned, Mary asked rather matter-of-factly what was up (vv 29-34). She wanted to know how He intended for it to become a reality.

Here is where we make our mistake and fail to get the wind of God beneath our wings. We do not ask for an explanation of what is required of us nor do we seek to get the bigger picture so we can govern ourselves accordingly. What are you working on right now? Do you have all the answers or a clear enough vision to press ahead? Or are there some missing pieces, people who need to be put in position or resources that need to be attained before going any further?

In all of Mary's querying, she got what she was looking for. In verse 35 we see a major change of countenance for Mary with the angelic discussion. The angel lets her know that she is not going to be handling her assignment alone.

When God sends the presence and power of the Holy Spirit to our aid, we become the crème that rises to the top.

No more uncertainty or uncomfortable conversations. No more issues surrounding our value and self-worth. Just God! His wind giving power under our wings!

The amazing turnaround begins when the dust settles from the chaos of our lives. In verse 38, Mary does two extraordinary things. She accepts that she is God's child to be used by Him at His discretion and she agrees to be the vessel God desires to use. And the journey for Mary as the mother of Jesus begins.

So it is with us. Once we accept and agree with God about the plans He has for us, then and only then will the road we travel be paved with God's unmerited favor.

Our faith will often endure the trials and hardships of our own scrutiny and the disbelief of others. If that were not the case would it be faith? You will get through to your next accomplishment in life by knowing you are a chosen vessel of God; that your case has been stated before Him and you are willing to be used in the capacity for which your life has been destined and ordained.

You can begin your personal empowerment process with these three simple steps:

1. **End personal quarreling and bickering with others.**
   (James 4:1 – 3)

2. **Honor the resources God sends to meet your needs.**
   (Philippians 4:19; Romans 8:32)

3. **Trust the promises and Word of God.**
   (Romans 10:17; Psalm 68:19)

The Joy of Discipline

You may be ready to walk in the way of God, but without discipline, you will have a difficult time attaining the greatness He has for you.

Discipline is the ability to stick to a thing by going through spiritual, mental, physical and emotional training. All of your faculties must be intact to reach your goals. Discipline allows us to soar above our situations.

Must we always be backed into a corner before we come out fighting? Or would it serve us better to instill the necessary disciplined behaviors to champion whatever comes our way before the challenge gets to us? On your walk to fulfillment, think about these areas of discipline that may require closer attention:

- **People skills.** *"Do not withhold good from those who deserve it, when it is in your power to act. Don't say to your neighbor, Come back later; I'll give it tomorrow; when you now have it with you."* - Proverbs 3:27-29

- **Leadership.** *"For a man's ways are in full view of the Lord, and he examines all his paths."* Proverbs 5:21

- **Relationships.** *"The integrity of the upright guides them, but the unfaithful are destroyed by their duplicity."* Proverbs 11:3

- **Temperament.** *"Like a city whose walls are broken down is a man who lacks self-control."* Proverbs 25:28

- **Business savvy.** *"The blessing of the Lord brings wealth, and he adds no trouble to it."* Proverbs 10:22

- **Communication.** *"Pleasant words are a honeycomb, sweet to the soul and healing to the bone."* Proverbs 16:24

- **Entanglement.** *"A gossip betrays a confidence; so avoid a man who talks too much."* Proverbs 20:19

- **...all "isms".** *"Each heart knows its own bitterness, and no one else can share its joy."* Proverbs 14:10

A life that has discipline is able to focus and express itself in ways never thought possible. Allow yourself to think about what God is doing and how He has been preparing you all along for the journey on which you now find yourself. For it is written, *"many are the plans in a man's heart, but it is the Lord's purpose that prevails."* (Proverbs 19:21)

Waiting for the Wind

Having the wind of the Lord beneath your wings gives you the ability to soar above debilitating circumstances and misplaced aspirations. As the power of God gives credibility to your projects, financial revenue streams to your hopes and strengthens relationships among family members, may you also come to appreciate the art of waiting on God (Psalm 37:7-9).

When we wait on God it does not mean we are standing idly by. While we wait we are actively preparing for what the Lord has in store for us.

While in a business seminar the leader stated four "P's" to successful business practices: *planning, preparation, promotion, participating.* As a Christian I learned very quickly how these four business strategies would also help me in daily living.

As I have grown, I added to the list: *prayer*. I have discovered that prayer must be the central focus of my endeavors. Prayer allows me to concentrate on the intricate details while never losing sight of the big picture. Each of the small steps leads me closer to my intended goals.

His Wind, Your Wings

The law of empowerment has conditions that must be adhered to if you are to receive the full power of God's presence in your life. They are:

> **Staying close to God.** *"If you abide in me, and my word abides in you, you shall ask whatever you will, and it shall be done."* (John 15:7)

> **Ridding your life of known sins.** *"If I regard iniquity in my heart, the Lord will not hear me."* (Psalm 66:18)

> **Asking in Jesus' name.** *"Whatever you ask in my name, and I will do it."* (John 16:23)

> **Seeking life according to God's will.** *"If you believe you will receive whatever you ask."* (Matthew 21:22)

> **Staying humble.** *"If my people who are called by name would humble themselves, and pray, seek my face and turn from their wicked ways, then I will hear from heaven, forgive their sin and heal their land."* (2 Chronicles 7:14)

What an awesome responsibility. Are you up for the challenge? I am. God will only get the best from me so that I can get the fullness of what He has to offer.

Three things will happen when these principles are applied to your life:

1. **You will be at peace.** *"And God will give you peace that surpasses all understanding."* (Philippians 4:7)

2. **You will have an opportunity to freely express your self.** *"Now Lord...enable your servants to speak your word with great boldness."* (Acts 4:29)

3. **You will sense God's presence in your life.** *"Where can I flee from your Spirit? Where can I flee from your presence?"* (Psalms 139:7)

God made you special. It's high time you got to doing what he has destined you to do!

Journaling: The Law of Empowerment

You are now ready to embark on the journey of a lifetime. You have the power of God on your side and the wisdom of His words in your Spirit. As you journal, allow your words to freely flow. Allow the Lord to lift you to a new level of appreciation for life.

Meditative Moments

As you prepare for your journey with God, take a few moments to quiet your mind, body and spirit. The balanced living technique is Meditation for Relaxation. We will begin with a simple relaxation pose, which can be done resting on the floor or lying in bed or lounging on the sofa.

This pose is a total relaxation while lying on your back. If you find any discomfort in your lower back or neck, place a rolled towel beneath your hips for support or use a pillow to support your neck. While lying still, pray for direction and guidance. Begin to take slow deep breaths through your nose. As you inhale and exhale discover your natural rhythm and allow yourself to concentrate on being free.

Benefits:

- Calms the mind and helps relieve stress and mild depression

- Relaxes the body

- Reduces headache, fatigue, and insomnia

- Helps to lower blood pressure

Prayer focus: Those seeking to live empowered lives.

Date _____

Heavenly insight you have gained:

List a personal quality you are learning about yourself.

List two positive words of affirmation to speak into your life. Write what you anticipate to happen in your life from these words.

List the names of three people who you will encourage today. Purposely seek them out in order to enrich their lives with your influence.

Balanced Living Time

More and more doctors are prescribing meditation and yoga (a form of stretching) as a way to lower blood pressure, improve exercise performance in people with heart conditions, help people with asthma breathe easier, relieve insomnia and generally relax from the everyday stresses of life. Because yoga is not a religion, but a practice for those who are religious or spiritual, we as believers can embrace the teachings of the ancients without conflict of our belief in God.

Learning to Appreciate Yourself

God admonishes us to meditate on his word day and night. As you journal consider basic breathing to relax you for your journey ahead. Meditation is a proven relaxation therapy. When we pray, take extended walks, listen to the smooth sound of jazz, or focus on positive affirmations, we are causing the relaxation of the mind, body and spirit.

There are various forms of meditation. By definition, meditation is a prayer form involving silent concentration. It just so happens that there are many forms to practice. To meditate from a Christian perspective is to use what is called a mantra. A mantra is the use of repetition of a song, word or phase that causes clarity to arise on part of the issue we are seeking guidance. Scripture, God, Christ, the Holy Spirit, songs from hymn books, the chorus of your favorite Gospel song, and personal prayers become the point of reference. Each of these resources, when utilized effectively, provides a sense of well-being and harmony.

I have selected a practice passage to use to get you started. You can use many types of literature to practice your reflective reading and application process. These are the words to a song by Rev. Timothy Wright and it simply says "Jesus, Jesus, Jesus, Jesus, Jesus, Jesus, Jesus, Jesus, Jesus, Jesus, Jesus, Jesus". Anyone who knows that song understands that the words are said over and over again, but in a different tone. The next words are "Thank you, thank you, thank you, thank you, thank you, thank you, thank you, thank you, thank you, thank you, thank you, thank you. Followed by as many times of Savior, Savior, Savior (repeat on). The video is provided by the Jordan Entertainment Group. It is known as the Katrina Song in honor of those who suffered greatly during Hurricane Katrina. It is available on YouTube. You can also learn of the incredible loss that the Wright family suffered just a few years after this song. There is a sure way to know that God is real and that He is active in your life. And there are several other ways to be definitive about what and how to build on and maintain a Christian life foundation.

Each day millions of people practice meditation. From time to time confusion arises as to whether or not Christians should practice meditation, yoga and other forms of spirituality that balance and focus our lives. As a Certified Yoga Instructor, practitioner, facilitator and teacher of relaxation, meditation and deep breathing techniques, I cannot express how important it is for the believer to use meditation as a way to get closer to God, themselves and their loved ones. Not only do I practice, I design rooms in homes, spas and office buildings to be used as places of meditation and relaxation. In our busy world, we all need a place to find solace and serenity.

For anyone looking to facilitate or practice meditation, it is important to be sure that integrity is shown above anything else.

As you are preparing for your journey, please read these scriptures in order to secure your position about the art of meditation. As a believer always use scripture as your guide as not to be led into areas where you are not ready to go. Read Deuteronomy 4:7, 2 Chronicles 7:14; Matthew 26;36; Luke 22:30-40; Romans 8:26; Psalm 119:15; Psalm 119:78; Psalm 119:97; Psalm 145:5; Psalm 1:1-2 and Psalm 104:34. Allow these scriptures to lead you to a new level in your faith and walk with the Lord.

Four Basics for Beginning Meditation

A quiet place.   The best environment for the practice of meditation is a quiet room, whether it is a bedroom, bathroom or large closet. Sometimes just the quiet simplicity in a car or elevator can assist with alleviating stress and tension. Move to a quiet place with minimum distractions. The object is to prepare the mind for a state of relaxation.

A comfortable position.   The postures most conductive to achieving relaxation are sitting in a chair, lying or sitting on the floor or kneeling. In traditional meditation postures, however, the back is normally kept erect, though not rigidly upright. This is called poised posture. The right attitude for meditation may itself be described as poised: alert yet also relaxed. Poised posture promotes the right state of attention-awareness for successful meditation.

An object upon which to dwell.   Often focusing on your own breathing creates awareness, fulfilling an element required for meditating for relaxation.   Some meditation methods involve looking at objects with open eyes, but in others, the eyes are closed which makes relaxation easier, if visualization is a part of your guided meditation process. An individual may choose a sound or phase or prayer. Repetition of a neutral word or praise is effective for Christian mantra meditation. Consider a word like *peace*, which has relaxing associations. If you make awareness of breathing your single meditation method, let your attention dwell on the gentle flow of air as it passes from your lungs and then out of your mouth or nose. As your breathing becomes quiet and more focused you will notice how the gentle rhythm promotes relaxation.

A positive perspective. A positive attitude is a staple of meditation for relaxation. When you are alert, yet not rigid, a keen sense of mental clarity is achievable. With practice, you will learn to summon at will incredible states of readiness and balance.

As you grow stronger in the Lord and your faith, it is my prayer that you will allow the Lord to guide you in to all truth about His word, your life and his will for your life. May the meditation practices represented here bring you comfort and joy in these stressful times.

I have found peace in God through His word and practices. Biblical holistic meditations will provide you with guidance, comfort and the fulfillment for which you are searching.

Everyday you will find hope for your present situation. You will receive healing from your past experiences and you will discover ways to lay a foundation for a spiritually prosperous heritage. I pray that you will discipline yourself to read affirming material each day and listen to the Lord speak to you at the point of your need. As you read you will find that writing allows your thoughts to pour from your soul to minister to your spirit.

May the grace and peace of God be yours both now and forever! Amen

Covenant

I will trust God to lead and guide me daily into all truth about every aspect of my life.

Name _____Date _____

Balanced Living Book Club
Session Tips

The Law of Perception

Discussion Questions

- [ ] What do you believe about God?
- [ ] Do you believe in God? Spiritual things?
- [ ] What is important to you now?
- [ ] What was important a year ago? Five? Ten?
- [ ] What things of importance have been consistent through the years?

Facilitator

- [ ] Engage your group in Q & A discussion about what is important to them.
- [ ] Dialogue with them about areas in their life that may have shaped their present views.
- [ ] Discuss with them how over time we build the basis of our foundation based on our beliefs.

The Law of Promise

Discussion Questions

- [ ] In what ways have broken promises impacted your life?
- [ ] Are you a person of your word?
- [ ] Why is integrity important?
- [ ] Do you depend on God in various aspects of your life?

- [ ] How so?
- [ ] Has God ever let you down? Why do you feel it was God?

Facilitator

- [ ] Introduce your participants to the concepts of truth and integrity.
- [ ] Allow students to volunteer to share their experiences with disappointment that stemmed from broken promises.
- [ ] Engage your group in a praise session on how good it felt when someone came through for them like they said they would.
- [ ] Seek to dispel any myths or half-truths or lies about God letting people down. Know for certain that God is faithful and will do what He says.
- [ ] Facilitators know your stuff. Stick to scripture.

The Law of Thanksgiving

Discussion Questions

- [ ] List three to seven things you would like to thank God for.
- [ ] What has been standing in your way that you did not have time to give thanksgiving to God?
- [ ] Have you been able to map out what it took to get you where you are? What do you see?
- [ ] Who have you failed to appreciate or give kudos to some one for helping you out? Doing a good job? Standing in the gap?

Facilitator

- [ ] The important thing is to not take God for granted.

- ☐ Lead your group into the knowledge that God expects us to thank Him.
- ☐ Talk to your group or lead in a discussion on worship.
- ☐ What is worship?
- ☐ How to worship.
- ☐ The names of God.

The Law of Commitment

Discussion Questions

- ☐ In the Law of Perception questions you listed a few things of importance to you. How committed are you to each of them?
- ☐ What things have you started that you abandoned?
- ☐ Why did you abandon them?
- ☐ What would happen to your life if God abandoned your requests?
- ☐ Why is commitment of value and importance?

Facilitator

- ☐ Open by giving a short testimony of one thing you are committed to and how you gave it to God so that it would be a success.
- ☐ Allow others to share. Let them know that some things maybe still be in the works; encourage them to share what ever they would like.
- ☐ Ask the group if they see how something they started, failed because they did not commit it to God first.
- ☐ Have a discussion on how things may have worked out differently if they had exercised Proverbs 16:3.

The Law of Harmony

Discussion Questions

- [ ] How do you make an effort to get along with others?
- [ ] What ways do you vent frustration?
- [ ] Do you let your negative emotions get the best of you?
- [ ] What are you doing to get your emotions under control?
- [ ] What are a few of your favorite scriptures?
- [ ] What positive emotions do those scriptures invoke?

Facilitator

- [ ] Open discussion with why scripture plays an important role in the life of the believer.
- [ ] As the facilitator or group leader you should be aware of particular scriptures that lead to positive emotional responses either toward oneself, God and/or others.
- [ ] Allow participants to discuss one of their favorite scriptures. As they recite it let them tell what positive emotional response it invokes.

The Law of Readiness

Discussion Questions

- [ ] How many times in your life have you been blind-sided?
- [ ] Name a specific incident that really opened your eyes to the reality of your situation.
- [ ] What did you learn, or are learning from this experience?
- [ ] Have you changed your pattern of behavior? Or do you still leap before you look?

Facilitator

- ☐ Talk to your group about readiness.
- ☐ There are four classes of people in the world.
- ☐ Give your group an opportunity to assess where they are and where they would like to be by using the following categories.

Ready and Willing. The person is prepared for what they have to accomplish in life and is taking the proper steps.

Willing and Unready. The person has the desire to move forward, but is lacking the skill and/or emotional prowess to pull it off.

Unwilling and Ready. The person has the physical ability and skill level to master the task, but is emotionally uncommitted.

Unready and Unwilling. The person is not prepared in any capacity to accept responsibility and move to the next level.

Talk to your group about spiritual gifts, talents and skill levels. Help them understand and comprehend the dynamics of mental ability and physical aptitude.

The Law of Creativity

Discussion Questions

- ☐ If you could start over, what would you do differently with your life?
- ☐ What do you feel has honestly kept you from achieving your dreams?

- [ ] How does your lack of initiative play a role in your ineffectiveness?
- [ ] What are you good at doing?
- [ ] Name a time you were ready to get out there and show the world that you could do it?

Facilitator

- [ ] Talk to your group about initiative and how some things in life seem to come naturally.
- [ ] Help your group to understand destiny.
- [ ] Be aware in your discussions if your participants talk about how others stopped them from achieving.
- [ ] Work with your group on owning up to their mistakes and getting past them.
- [ ] Encourage your group to be courageous on their future attempts.

The Law of Empowerment

Discussion Questions

- [ ] What is God trying to get your attention about?
- [ ] Has the Lord been preparing and leading you to try something new or revive your present skills?
- [ ] In what ways is being empowered uplifted your spirits?
- [ ] How does the story of Esther inspire you?
- [ ] How does the story of Mary inspire you?

Facilitator

- [ ] Talk to your group about taking the opportunities of God that are presented to them.

☐ Involve your group in a discussion about feeling free to go the next level of life.

☐ Openly discuss with your group how the presence and power of God is theirs and that they can achieve their dreams, great and small.

I pray these meeting times have been a blessing to you. I pray more and more of Gods' grace will fall upon you as you let the Lord have his way in your life.

A Message to the Facilitator

Journaling is an important part of the Christians life. When we journal we are able to express our thoughts, fears, joys and overall concern about life in general, yet in specific terms. As a facilitator you will be asked to offer insight on the principles for that week, the participants' misgivings about God and scripture and also help them make peace with what is and has been happening in their lives. I am excited that you are leading in this venue. I know that as you lead you will find yourself asking hard questions and seeking answers that only God can give. It is my prayer that for your series of group meetings you will be open, honest and loving toward yourself and those in your group.

You can meet for one hour to two hours depending on the size and participation of your group. Your group can be any age level or marital status. Consider letting everyone volunteer one or two of their favorite insights to share at each meeting.

As they share their stories be sure to find out what they learned through the journaling process and how God is working on their behalf. As the group leader you may start sharing or solicit in advance one or two people to start off sharing to help the others feel safe and comfortable.

Remember to open and close each meeting with prayer. There will be times when what is shared is painful and personal. You will want to remind the group that everything is confidential and should not be shared without permission.

Praise Rally

In your final group meeting each participating group may come together for a time of prayer, praise and testimony. Each group should enlist four to five people to share what they have learned and to briefly say how the journaling experience has caused them to focus more on listening to and having quality time with God. They may also be open to sharing how relationships with others have improved because of their awareness of other's feelings and the release of past baggage.

Be Fulfilled!

About the Author

Jacquie Hood Martin, an ordained minister, and sought after international speaker. She is chief spiritual officer of Jacquie Hood Ministries, serving leaders for more nearly twenty years by providing Christian Life Skills coaching, training, teaching and preaching to pastors and their congregations.

Hood Martin, a longtime national trainer for LifeWay Christian resources, and served a decade as the first female staff pastor at The Church Without Walls in Houston, Texas, founded by Dr. Pastor Ralph Douglas West, Sr. She is currently a resident minister, while she serves as Co-Pastor of The Bridge Network International, Chicago, IL.

She received her theological training from Southwestern Baptist Theological Seminary in Houston, Texas, which positioned her for radio bible ministry and other outreach opportunities. She has earned Bachelor and Masters degrees in Religion and Christian Communication. Hood Martin is pursuing a doctoral degree in Higher Education. At the printing of this book, she has been recently appointed as Vice President of Academic Affairs and Student Services within the City Colleges of Chicago Community College System.

Hood Martin is married to Roland S. Martin, Talk Show host of Washington Watch with Roland Martin, TV-One Cable News Network, Syndicated Columnist, Author, and part of the best Political Team on television, CNN.

Recommended reading

Who Moved My Cheese, Spencer Johnson, M.D.
The Success Journey: The Process of Living Your Dreams, John Maxwell
The Celebration of Discipline, Richard Foster
The Life God Blesses; Weathering the Storms that Conquer the Soul, Gordon MacDonald
Rich Minds, Rich Rewards, Valorie Burton
The Nature of a True Diva, LaRita Shelby
Children Learn What They Live, Dorothy Law Nolte and Rachel Harris
Only a Woman, Terri McFaddin
Standing Tall, Steve Farr
Midlife Clarity: Epiphanies from grown-Up Girls, Cynthia Black and Laura Carlsmith
Be Restored!, Debra Berry
The One Minute Manager, Kenneth Blanchard, PhD and Spencer Johnson, M.D.
Knight in Shining Armor, P.B. Wilson
Point Man, Steve Farr
Anchor Man, Steve Farr
Having What Matters, Monique Greenwood
Taking Over, Bishop Eddie L. Long
Five Temptations of a CEO, Patrick Lencioni
Seven Spiritual Laws of Success, Deepak Chopra
Light on Yoga, B.K.S. Iyengar
Yoga for Wellness, Gary Kraftsow

Fulfilled!
The Art and Joy of Balanced Living

ORDER FORM
You can order online at www.jacquiehood.com

Organization Name:

_____

Your Name:

_____

Address:

_____

City, State

_____

Zip Code

_____

Telephone Number

_____

E-Mail Address:

_____

PRICE SCHEDULE

1-4 Books: $12.95
5-9 Books: $11.95
25-99 Books: $9.95
100 + Books: $8.95

Price is for each book in each category.

YOUR ORDER

Number of book(s) ordered ___ x price per book ___= _____

Sales tax for books shipped to Texas address only   _____
Texas address only (multiply total order by 8.25%)

Shipping is $3.50 for one book; $1.50 for each   _____
Additional book

Total Cost   _____

Make checks payable to NuVision Media, Inc.-- Additional
information is available online.

Allow three (3) weeks for delivery. If you have any questions,
send an e-mail to Jacquie@jacquiehood.com.

Organizations or groups ordering 50 or more books will receive a
complimentary 2-hour Balanced Living Seminar. For additional
details, please contact us at Jacquie@jacquiehood.com.

Balanced Living Seminars

As a Christian Life Skills coach people have come up to speak very openly with me about private issues they face. After prayerful consideration we realized that thousands of others could benefit from their questions and Christ's answers given to me for them. Consider a seminar, intensive or weekend retreat to meet the growing need of people whose lives are out of balance because of past situations. Remember, proactive is better than reactive.

Balanced Living through the A, B, C's of Life…
Balanced Living through Abortion
Balanced Living through Broken Relationships
Balanced Living through Conflict and Confusion
Balanced Living through Deception
Balanced Living through Employment
Balanced Living through Family Issues
Balanced Living through Gangs and Guns
Balanced Living through Homosexuality
Balanced Living through Incest
Balanced Living through Joblessness
Balanced Living through Kids and Marital Issues
Balanced Living through Lustful Thinking
Balanced Living through Marriage and Menopause
Balanced Living through Neediness
Balanced Living through Obesity
Balanced Living through Pain and Suffering
Balanced Living through Quiet Time
Balanced Living through Rape
Balanced Living through Surgery
Balanced Living through Terminal Illness
Balanced Living through Unforeseen Circumstances
Balanced Living through Violent Acts
Balanced Living through Widowhood
Balanced Living through X Y Z…name your need!